How I Committed Suicide

How I Committed Suicide

A REVERIE

C. L. Sulzberger

NEW HAVEN AND NEW YORK
TICKNOR & FIELDS
1982

Designed by Sally Harris / Summer Hill Books

Library of Congress in Publication Data

Sulzberger, C. L. (Cyrus Leo), 1912-
How I committed suicide.
1. Suicide. I. Title.
HV6545.S86   306   81–14555
ISBN 0–89919–054–5   AACR2

Printed in the United States of America

V 10 9 8 7 6 5 4 3 2 1

The author is grateful for permission to quote from *The Naked Ape* by Desmond Morris. Copyright © by Desmond Morris. Used with the permission of McGraw-Hill Book Company.

For Christopher
who tries so hard to understand

Contents

ONE 🌿 The Keys to My Prison

The dawn I committed suicide burst with such splendor and magnificent beauty that, at the last moment, I would have called off the terrible deed had I been able. But I had already shot dead my dearest, most faithful, most adoring friend as he looked at me squarely with the most lovely and most trustful eyes the world has ever known.

It was that phase in planetary geography when the moon was at its perigee. As the sun slid silently upward out of the eastward island crags the last phosphorescent ripples of the night wavered across the whispering sea and faded into the fulvous, ever broader solar path painted along the tranquil water.

Spring was just starting to blossom across Spetsais with its usual fury. Christopher and I had spent the entire previous afternoon — our last for all eternity — wandering across the mountain. The customarily arid, rocky fields were covered with tall green wheat into which he disappeared from time to time, hidden in his own verdant Douanier-Rousseau jungle. His progress discernible only by a ripple amid the swelling grain, he moved forward like a tiny, velvet-eared storm of happiness; diagonal zigzags of joy never geodetically predictable.

He had lunched well and with gusto; carrots and mutton, with the bone. Gaiety marked his every movement. He bounded out of rustling confines past a herdsman's shieling into the cleared spaces cropped by fat sheep ready for the shears. Everywhere were clusters of bright yellow, lavender, white, and pink wild flowers, and tiny red anemones; all exquisitely framed by the luxurious blossoms of orange and almond trees, the solemn pines and elegant cypresses that, in the Mediterranean basin, are generally associated with death. And in my loneliness I thought of John Donne's reflection in *Biathanatos*: "Mee thinks I have the keyes of my prison in mine owne hand, and no remedy presents it selfe so soone to my heart, as mine own sword."

There is but one cure to that marcescent loneliness which comes with age and which brings with it the realization that human proximity is the equivalent of arteriosclerosis while human absence is the equivalent of death. I have family and friends of whom I am fond but they are not here, I reflected, and Christopher Beagle is my only warm, living, true and understanding daily confidant. How right Donne was, I thought, except it was mine own gun and not my sword. And Christopher must go with me, as he would insist, even into drear infinity, as he had been with me in so many pleasanter places.

That final afternoon, I sat upon a flat chunk of conglomerate and watched the moon rise between a cypress and a cypress. I wondered why the ancient Greeks were so different from other Mediterranean peoples, never greeting such natural events in fear or by blowing frightened, wailing music through conch shells or on ram's-horn trumpets, but saluting them joyously: both the glorious sun and the waterless, lifeless moon which controls the tides of our seas and the spasms of womanly creation.

The sun is, of course, the quintessential life symbol of the early animists and the moon its antithesis, death; and certainly the earliest Proto-Helladic people were, like all other simple, naive folk, influenced by animism. But they seemed to derive more exuberance from life, and less sorrow from its inevitable conclusion, than those other strange and exhilarating communities that lined these shores. The ancient Greeks were more enthralled by life and less obsessed with death than the Egyptians to the south. In this respect the audacious Cretans, who toyed with death by somersaulting over charging bulls, represented a psychological as well as geographical frontier between two famous civilizations.

Killing, indeed, was — and still is — a frequently exposed facet of the Hellenic character. As far as I know, Homer is the earliest to recount the head-hunting exploits of Greek warriors in their civil war at Troy (inspired, according to Aeschylus, by overpopulation on these barren, unproductive soils, and therefore arranged by the gods to pare "an insolent abundance" of people). But head-hunting still prevails, having occurred as recently as World War II. Then, during their civil conflict, government bounty hunters were paid a piece-rate fee for every head of an *andarte* guerrilla, male or female, which, after it was bought and paid for, was exposed on village pickets.

Nevertheless, killing is an act; not the same thing as the state of cold, abstract death. It manufactures death; it creates it; but it is, in its violent way, a frenzied expression of life. It is the sun, which can burn to nothingness with its life-giving energy. Death, the result, is the cold, indifferent moon.

Since childhood I have been much possessed by death, neither admiring nor fearing it but regarding it with respect. Only one adjective lends itself to death; it is final. It is not kind, good, evil, cruel, blessed, long, short, squalid, benign or lovely. It is so powerful as to be indifferent: like the law of gravity, wherever in space it applies; or like infinity or eternity, which mean much the same and may, indeed, both be combined in Einstein's first theory, about the fifth dimension.

Dying is generally unpleasant and often agonizing. But death is otherwise — every man's parent, it makes of all humans identical twins. Whether they were born in the age of pharaonic Egypt, Periclean Athens, Confucian China or Renaissance Italy, each in due time died and became indistinguishable, one from the other: as dust they acquired precisely the same age. Moses is no older than Lenin although they were born over three thousand years apart in what we know as time. Each came from nowhere and went back to nowhere and the infinity that preceded their origin is equaled only by the infinity which accepted their return into its arms.

Age does not exist for death and, while death is a part of life, always tiptoeing along its edges if not thundering across it, life has no part whatsoever of or in death. Death is always ready to embrace man and many men have despaired of this potential, yet all have it. One cannot choose to be born but one can choose when to die, if the choice is not exaggerated in terms of greedy and egotistic ambition; of attempting to outlive one's time.

For death is always lurking there, so mighty that it is unaware of its own existence; of the terror it has aroused among billions merely by its contemplation as an idea; of the fact that its mere presence forever among us has given rise to beautiful legends and frightening myths, and to gods and religions who promised their foolish advocates they would do away with or elude this totally terminal force. For to death, men are wholly meaningless. Algae, Alexandrian, or alguazil; Socialist, Socrates, or Socinian; edelweiss, Edam, or Edison — all are devoured in that insatiable and invisible maw.

What men can do to escape death's immutable anonymity — and that but for a mere flash of time — is to pass on something of good with their otherwise meaningless lives. The algae feeds the krill which feeds the whale; although all die. Pericles, Plato, and Phidias bequeathed great beauty to succeeding generations before succumbing to numb invisibility. Blind Homer and flashing Shakespeare joined Botticelli and Bach in making future lives agreeable. But where will their works be an unknown number of eons from now? Transported to another planet? And then, to yet another? And in the end: nowhere. At home, together in the fold of anonymous, unadjectival death.

Sitting upon a Greek rock and watching a merry, inquisitive little dog playing on a warm, spring-clad hillside one tends to reflect on the life one is preparing to leave. I do not know — although soon I shall find out — whether in the last moments of one's existence one relives the years about to terminate, relives them like a cinematic film run in a brief flick at a million times its usual pace. But I do know that, in this sadly pleasant atmosphere, one can regretfully inspect what one has done with the time awarded by sheer chance to endure quite consciously one's own momentary flick through impassive eternity.

I suppose most lives are failures because they do not satisfy the tenant of what are called one's body and one's soul. I now see, gazing over Christopher's proudly curled, caducean white tail, following his wiggling rear through thorny bushes, that I have spent my time not living but existing, not doing but watching. When Marina died I acutely knew what true love was — when it was no longer available to give or to receive. And the hollow of that experience has grown steadily and heavily as the initial shock that carved it out of me has wearily eroded.

My mature existence was as a journalist, which professionally requires much trouble and a wide acquaintanceship. Only too, too late — old and retired — did I realize that hanging around intellectuals doesn't make one an intellectual; hanging around great men in the capacity of recorder of their greatness doesn't raise one from the ruck of mediocrity; hanging around wars doesn't make one a warrior (or brave) any more than hanging around revolutions makes one a revolutionist.

Maybe it is honest to acknowledge one is a failure in this, the only life one will ever enjoy (endure?), but there is little satisfaction in truth of this glum sort. It is precisely the equivalent of discovering to one's displeasure that one is a woefully committed atheist and, moreover, that such an anticredo is in no slightest sense a substitute for the faith one cannot manage to discover. Nonreligion is no religion. One may seek to live this stark life according to a code of ethics as conceived by dead philosophers but while there may be smug satisfaction in any small success produced by such efforts, there is no comfort in a minor achievement of this sort.

Indeed, it enhances the awareness that there is no comfort whatsoever in solitude, a solitude that distances one from his fellows on this earth and from the very concept of that divinity which eases the sorrowful path of so many others. It is sad to find oneself an atheist who bleakly if firmly believes in neither a past nor a future life and, therefore, may more keenly than most regret the inadequacy of his own experience on the fringes of existence. But what can be more remote than regret?

Do not ask me why I am an atheist. I have had many deeply religious friends, including more than one priest, of differing faiths and on more than one occasion each has made the inquiry I find impossible to answer. My parents were agnostic, perhaps even atheists; but they did not say so. By nationality I am American and my family — refugees like all my countrymen (including the Indians whom we turned into refugees) — first came to my homeland three centuries ago. By race I am a Jew (although most Jews refuse the racial categorization) and in my veins I know as far as it is possible to know such things, that not one single drop of non-Jewish blood runs. And by religion I am an atheist. I have told my children (whose mother was a Christian) that if anyone asks them their religion they should answer "Jewish" — no matter what they actually believe — until it becomes chic and fashionable to be a Jew, which is not yet the case. But that is a matter of pride, a kind of ego trip; it is no faith.

Perhaps I am one of the few practicing atheists (does one, indeed, "practice" a noncredo?) who attended classes at a divinity school. When I was a junior at Harvard, Hitler seized power in Germany making me, for the first time, keenly aware of what it meant to be a Jew. So, although I was already doing research for my thesis on why John Donne took orders in the Church of England (quitting Roman Catholicism to do so), I took courses in Jewish history and theology given by a famous professor of religion.

I found no answers. Yet I was amused that, although almost all my fellow students were preparing for the priesthood in one or another sect, several among them, perhaps still less moral than they hoped to become, availed themselves of the opportunity I willingly abetted to crib from my papers.

The experience served well to remind me of the long and burdensome heritage of Jewry and inspired in my mind a question never satisfactorily answered: what is the reason for anti-Semitism, and why is it a phenomenon only in Europe, its erstwhile colonies (including the Americas), and the Islamic world; not in the Orient? The experience did nothing, I may add, to lessen my atheistic belief.

My life, which is now about to end abruptly, has had its own rewards, although few of what might be called a public nature. I have declined those decorations proffered me, and also what I believed improper favors, such as a Greek millionaire's suggestion that I borrow his yacht for a fortnight and invite my family and friends on a cruise. He thought I was loony when I demurred, saying I could not properly place myself under any obligation to him. The shipowner promptly reproffered it to Allen Dulles, then head of the CIA, who gleefully accepted. This attitude, my wife reminded me, may be satisfying to the soul but is rarely advantageous. Marina liked yachts more than I.

Elsewhere, I attempted to memorialize that adorable woman after her death in 1976, using her own words to shape a picture of her entrancing personality and soul. I have also recounted some four decades of history as I, on my miniscule scale, have observed it as a camera might. However, as much as possible, I have kept my uninteresting self out of these recollections. Now, on the threshold of nothingness, I put down not only the thoughts of my very best friend (who, alas, is unable to write them himself) but also my thoughts on him.

So, looking down from my mountain perch over the whitewashed houses, the cheerful little sails and the gleaming blue sea; listening to the scratching noise as a puzzled Christopher gingerly paws the shell of a heavily armored tortoise, I turn my mind to the life we are both about to quit and to the nothingness ready to accept us. And I wonder not only, egocentrically, about ourselves, but what will be left of Earth a few years, decades, or generations hence.

Will it be inherited by seven-year locusts whose well-buried eggs may be interred long enough to survive the swirls of drifting fallout from nuclear explosions? Or by the wingless mosquitoes discovered thousands of feet below the Antarctic ice, whose eggs can be hatched into live creatures centuries after they are laid, a rudimentary confirmation of the pseudoscience of cryonics? Or will mankind by the time it commits mass suicide in this world, have preceded the event by exporting to another planet a rocketed new Noah's Ark containing at least the elements of future self-sufficiency and a few human couples (as well as beagles)?

The essence of life in Greece is argument, just as the essence of death anywhere is silence. Socrates wrote in *Phaedo*: "There is one danger that we must guard against . . . of becoming misologic, in the sense that people become misanthropic. No greater misfortune could happen to anyone than that of developing a dislike for argument." (As I have done virtually since I was born, making me eligible to leave Greece and life, both disputatious.)

The maieutic Socrates was a great if highly irritating man. He knew truth, and for this his fellows condemned him to die. According to his pupil, Plato, a poet, mathematician, philosopher, and memoirist, Socrates cautioned his students:

Let me tell you gentlemen, that to be afraid of death is only another form of thinking one is wise when one is not; it is to think that one knows what one does not know. No one knows with regard to death whether it is not really the greatest blessing that can happen to a man; but people dread it as though they were certain it is the greatest evil; and this ignorance, which thinks it knows what it does not, must surely be ignorance most culpable.

Christopher has abandoned the tortoise and returned to look quizzically at me, his head slightly tilted. I say to him: "The desire to control one's death, to have a death of your own, is rare, even as rare as having a life of one's own. You are little and relatively young so you carry a small death within you. I am older and bigger so I carry a large death. But we are both ready to make use of this. We are both, after all, part of Marina's brief immortality and bear her living memory. If the two of us depart at the same instant we cut deeply into her eternity. But still there are the children and the grandchildren to carry on the thought of her and what she taught.

"At least she died with the knowledge that she had done so many good and kind things — as have you. I never achieved that noble aim, which is why my final years became so bitter. Remember, Christopher, her uninhibited and strangely daring private smile?

"And now we too are about to pass away and not a single soul will know it: just like two shooting stars that fall when nobody is looking or when the night is too cloudy to see them. Life, we will learn so soon, is revocable; death is not. Each life belongs to an individual: two, to the two of us. But death, not dying, is the common property of all. Therefore we must be modest."

This has bewildered Christopher, like much that I do and say, so as he trots off brimming with his endless inquisitiveness, I return to Socrates:

Death is one of two things. Either it is annihilation, and the dead have no consciousness of anything; or, as we are told, it is really a change: a migration of the soul from this place to another. Now if there is no consciousness but only a dreamless sleep, death must be a marvelous gain. I suppose that if anyone were told to pick out the night on which he slept so soundly as not even to dream, and then to compare it with all the other nights and days of his life, and then were told to say, after due consideration, how many better and

happier days and nights than this he had spent in the course
of his life — well, I think that the Great (Persian) King himself, to say nothing of any private person, would find these
days and nights easy to count in comparison with the rest.
If death is like this, then, I call it gain; because the whole of
time, if you look at it in this way, can be regarded as no more
than one single night.

If on the other hand death is a removal from here to some
other place, and if what we are told is true, that all the dead
are there, what greater blessing could there be than this,
gentlemen? . . . Put it in this way: how much would one of
you give to meet Orpheus and Musaeus, Hesiod and Homer?
I am willing to die ten times over if this account is true.

Only Marina; only to meet her! That, Christopher, would be
enough. If you understood me I am confident you would agree.
But it cannot be, despite the Athenian's sweet logic. And remember, as he said: "It would hardly be suitable for a man of my age
to resent having to die." Or, for that matter, to forsake you and
abandon you to the cold misery of solitude in an indifferent
world.

III   Marina believed there were only two complete
freedoms in life and one almost unconditional
one: "to love, to dream, and to take one's own
life." The "almost unconditional" referred to
suicide, which she thought was wholly legitimate and up to every
human to decide except if excluded by special obligations to those
who were psychologically or in other ways dependent on them.

A naturally cheerful and gregarious extrovert, she occasionally thought about death, but with regret, not fear. Sixteen
years before her own demise she wrote me: "Don't let's die except together." In 1971 she said: "Ah me. If only one could pick

one's time for dying." In a letter to her mother the following year she confided: "I must say it's grim to be getting to the deadable age."

I reflected on these sadly remembered observations as I whistled to Christopher and headed him further along the crest between rows of trees leading to the lonely chapel of Y Khara, a deserted house once tenanted by three old ladies but now by ghosts and birds. "You can explore for hares," I told him. Two years ago he had started one there and so I remarked: "Here, on your last afternoon, you may uncover at least the ghost of his scent while I sit in the coolth of that splendid shade and arrange my thoughts." *Y Khara* means "joy."

Unlike Marina, I have always contemplated death. Without it there could be no life; only the contrast explains mortality and makes one understand what living really means. Death is the antithesis of any form of being. Beside it all thoughts vanish. It is an infinity of greatness and of smallness: the greatness it encompasses after one's existence and the smallness it hugs tightly before that existence started. It is hard for a human brain to imagine, but that infinity of greatness is as large as all the boundless light-years of outer space compared to one tiny atom, and that infinity of smallness is just as miniaturized inside the components of that atom which is, to each other component, as endless as outer space is to itself.

More than twenty years ago I wrote a book called *My Brother Death*. I have seen death from childhood: grandparents, suicides, accidents. In Pittsburgh I began newspaper work as a reporter in the Alleghany County morgue and learned the cynicism of morticians as they stuffed and powdered corpses of different racial origins and prepared them for public display beneath glass to be recognized by relatives or friends. Those drowned bodies raked out of Pittsburgh's three rivers were photographed, fingerprinted (if possible) and dumped into a chemical tank.

I saw death when I was (by my own choice and after surreptitiously distributing bribes to Nazi officials) locked up in the

Zentral Friedhof (main mortuary) of nazified Vienna in early 1938. With a pencil torch I examined bodies listed in the ledgers as "suicides." But when I hauled the sheets back I was struck by the methodical illogic of the Nazis: never before had I heard of people killing themselves by beating out their own eyes.

Like millions of my generation I have seen death on battlefields: dead Americans, English, Germans, Italians, Greeks; large, long-robed Moroccan *goumiers* with their short, wicked knives, and miniature, affable looking Nepalese *ghurkas* clutching their long, sickle-shaped knives. And the most vividly remembered dead thing I ever saw, beautiful as some sad scene from the lovely old Welsh tale, *Mabinogion*, was a Russian horse mortally struck in the side, standing frozen stiff on the edge of a forest near Volokolamsk, the blood in its wound instantly congealed against the white snow in a bright red splash, not the rust color customary to corpses less recently slaughtered and in warmer climes.

Great men, like small men, give due attention to death in their private thoughts. Winston Churchill believed there was no form of afterlife, only some kind of velvety cool blackness. But, he added: "Of course I may be wrong. I might well be reborn as a Chinese coolie. In such a case, I should lodge a protest." When asked if he felt qualified for heaven he replied: "Surely the Almighty must observe the principles of English common law and consider a man innocent until proven guilty."

When he was very old, in his last year as German chancellor, but still erect, active and astute, I asked Konrad Adenauer if he would tell me precisely what he thought death was. He admitted to his own religiosity (his son was a Catholic priest) and then said: "No human knows the answer. If I could tell you that — but no one can. It is perhaps a gift of God that I myself have little if any fear. I think of death with equanimity.

"I cannot imagine that the soul, which is our life, could fade to nothing when death comes. Somehow it must continue to exist. Man is not permitted to know how — but it must. Because the origin of life, life itself, is as much of a mystery as death, we are unable to explain either phenomenon. The highest commandment has always been that which others hand on to us — to do one's duty."

Charles de Gaulle saw in death the harmonious completion of life and added: "Sophocles said that one must wait until the evening to see how splendid the day was; that one cannot judge life until death." When the aging general had returned to Paris from Churchill's funeral — a tremendous historical spectacle — I asked him whether its pomp and circumstance had incited him to make similar plans for himself. No, he answered.

It was indeed important and he had thought about it a good deal. But his funeral would be the opposite of Churchill's. "There will be no spectacle for de Gaulle," he concluded, referring to himself in the third person as he often did. This, of course, was not the case nor did he imagine as much. He was buried at his gloomy home village among wartime companions, but a massive memorial service attended by all the world's great was staged in Notre Dame.

When David Ben-Gurion, Israel's founder, was edging to death's doorstep, I asked him at his modest kibbutz home in the Negev Desert how he felt about the inevitable end. He said: "The purpose of life is to enjoy it, to make it pleasanter for every human being. We don't know of another world so we must concentrate on this one. People should be just and decent and loving. There is no mention in the Bible (the Old Testament) of an afterlife.

"Death is what it seems to be. But I don't know. Nobody knows. Once I talked about this to Einstein and he said: 'The more we progress in science, the more we realize what we don't know. Our ignorance increases; the riddle grows.' I asked him: 'Is there life after death?' He said: 'I wish I knew.' But remember, in his will he left orders that his body should be burned. I don't think he would come back again. Remember, there is no word in the Torah that concerns any other life."

Tito, an atheist and a vigorous, formidable man, bold and without fear, lived well into his eighties before he was stricken and then, to the world's embarrassed horror (thank heavens he was mostly unconscious) was kept alive by idiotic doctors — existing for weeks like some kind of mechanized turnip plugged into innumerable machines. But I already knew what he considered death and the purpose of life. Once he told me:

"Death depends on how one lives. If you have done something useful it will survive you. If someone has played a certain role in life, even then the world won't go downhill when he dies. What he has done for the good will remain. Much depends on what one has contributed to a country or a people. History is a long process. People never forget what was positive in the contribution of any leader. They will always remember what was good in his achievements. There is a proverb: 'Happy is the man who lives forever.' What this means is that he has done something good."

Of a subsequent generation, French president Valéry Giscard d'Estaing expressed to me the following views on death: "Of course, you know, I am a believer. Therefore I believe in survival. And, as a statesman, I expect that, normally speaking, I shall depart from my present position alive." (He was then, in late 1977, only fifty-one years old.)

"Consequently, there is no question about the effect of death upon me as a statesman — except for the wholly unforeseeable accident of something like an assassination. As for the judgment of history — I don't really think history will think of us. Time does not have much memory. Monuments are not important. But of course there will always be specialists, students of history, who will try to investigate what went on before."

What, I asked, did he hope to be remembered for in history? His answer was thoughtful, intelligent, and not suddenly blurted out but followed some reflection. He said: "A man must manage

his moment in history. I would like to be remembered as someone who made French democracy work well. There are many
people who have contributed in one or another way to this idea.
Also, many of them are not well known by the world at large.

"I wish — like Thomas Jefferson — to strengthen a function-
ing democracy that is able successfully to face the problems of
our own time and our own circumstances."

Somehow each of these leaders was saying in his own way
what the book Ecclesiastes, which they had probably all read,
even the total nonbeliever Tito, concludes wearily: "One generation passeth away, and another generation cometh: but the earth
abideth forever. . . . All go unto one place; all are dust, and all
turn to dust again."

Most humans now accept the idea of inevitable death although
for millions of them (Hindus) this means but an end to a present
state of existence succeeded by an endless progression of reincar-
nations and transmogrifications. And while the vast majority of
people prefer the thought of a gentle, painless end — perhaps
amid an ordinary night's sleep — the manner of dying can rarely
be controlled except in suicide. When this is the solution chosen,
Rainer Maria Rilke's concept of a "well-crafted death" assumes
special meaning. The German poet wrote in *The Notebook of Malte
Laurids Brigge*:

> Who, nowadays, cares for a well-crafted death? Nobody.
> . . . It is rare to find anyone who wishes to have a death of
> his own. . . . Long ago . . . one carried death within oneself
> the way the fruit carries the pit within itself. The children
> had a small one inside and the grown-ups a big one. The
> women carried it in their chest. One possessed it and there
> was a peculiar dignity and a quiet pride in this possession.

Suicide — intentional self-destruction — has been condemned
by the three great Middle Eastern religions: Judaism, Christianity, and Islam. The Talmud denounces it as sinful. Christianity

opposed it from the start with the argued exception of women killing themselves to avoid rape; and Saint Augustine firmly opposed even that. Yet, oddly enough, saints Francis the Seraphic, Radegonde, Martinien, Pacôme, and many others were canonized suicides. The Koran considers it an even greater crime than murder.

However, the Greeks permitted convicted criminals, like Socrates, to take their own lives and were not opposed to suicide as a means of escaping extreme disgrace or seizure by an enemy. India's Brahmins lavished praise on Hindu widows, who were expected to throw themselves upon the funeral pyres of their husbands. In Japan, *seppuku*, or self-disembowelment, was a ceremonial rite commended to honorable gentlemen. Certain Buddhist sects, especially in Southeast Asia, practice suicide by immolating themselves alive. Tertullian, Carthaginian lawyer and also a father of the Christian church, considered Jesus a suicide. It was only in A.D. 553 and A.D. 562 that church councils banned funeral rites to those who slew themselves. Yet even in the fourteenth and fifteenth centuries there were suicide waves among monks.

Practice varies not only in method but in geography, and clearly bears a relationship to climate and social factors in differing lands. Ireland has one of Europe's lowest suicide rates; Austria and Hungary among the highest; yet, all are Catholic. As people get older — especially men — the proportion of suicides increases markedly. Four times as many males over sixty-five kill themselves as young adults. And men commit suicide about four times as often as women who, by the way, make many more unsuccessful tries. Blacks apparently are far less suicidal than whites. In England, gas, poisoning, hanging, and drowning are the favorite means employed. In the United States shooting is the most popular method. Suicide numbers appear to increase everywhere in spring and early summer.

What the sociologist Emile Durkheim calls "egoistic suicide" stems from a lack of integration of any individual in society or a person without close interpersonal connections. Epicurus shrewdly discerned that sometimes fear of death drives men to kill themselves but Seneca considered suicide the "road to liberty." Saint Thomas regarded it as a special form of homicide. Goethe analyzed the process in his romantic novel, *Werther,* which stimulated an extraordinary tide of self-murder throughout mid-nineteenth-century Europe. Schopenhauer reasoned paradoxically that those who committed suicide thereby proved their desire to live. Marcus Aurelius wrote that he who considers suicide a crime is heedless that he closes what Seneca dubbed the roads to freedom.

From all these thoughts, I have long since concluded that, as an American male of the age-group where suicide is most prevalent, with few remaining close interpersonal connections and a lifelong preference for solitude, it is logical that I should decide to kill myself — and with a gun. But it must be a "well-crafted death" — for Christopher's sake and for those who survive us and are fond of us.

The Gauls often considered suicide a duty and the best means of achieving definitive happiness, above all as they approached old age. The Goths had an approving word for those who preferred death to elderly feebleness. The Celts promised an eternity of paradise to suicides. The closest retainers of the chiefs in all these pagan tribes slaughtered themselves with their wives as their leaders' corpses burned. For them suicide was an imposed and obligatory duty.

Strangely enough, even in the individualistic West, where religious ties are tending steadily to weaken, suicide is still generally regarded in the framework of acceptance that a human is able to kill himself but shouldn't do it. Nevertheless, it is estimated that nowadays about a thousand suicides occur in the world each day and twice as many are attempted at the same time but fail. Since 1789, when the French Revolution removed suicide from the list of penal crimes, it has become, in a sense, respectable in the Occident.

There is something almost schizophrenic about the pair of us, Christopher and I, musing in the loveliness of Y Khara's tree-lined paths. Christopher, although fully aware that strange thoughts are passing through my mind, is insistently sniffing, rushing about, making the most of this splendid afternoon with such a frenzy that I wonder if his extrasensory genius somehow hints to his nontime-keeping mind that this may be the last of such — or any — afternoons. And I, inactive and much more pensive, like the character out of Dostoyevsky, have "decided to kill myself in the Spring; this decision is connected with the kind of death I have chosen."

From the moment, as a child, when I first understood death's meaning and its personal implication — that I, a happy boy, was not and never could be immortal — I accepted the inevitable, if resentfully. I thought about it, with interest and not a little irritation, but I found that when I wished I could easily disengage and turn my mind to other more consolatory subjects.

Yet with the passage of time this became, as for everyone it becomes, more difficult. When death's immutable roll call began to rattle its muffled drumbeats bonily over my life, I understood its meaning: my grandfathers, my father, my grandmothers, my mother, my uncles, my closest friends, most dolefully my exuberant, happy wife.

Death's arrival is not always somber. There are cases when one says: "At last poor Jack has been released from agony." And there is a poetry in dying at one's peak, young but brimming with eagerness. Yet my personal roll call seems uniformly sorrowful.

I now understand why Marina's grandmother, Maria, an old lady in excellent health, willed herself to die at ninety-six. She was the last of her generation, wholly out of touch with its successors, devoutly religious, confident of a pleasant afterlife and impatient to continue, with long-dead relatives and friends, those deferred conversations to which she had always been accustomed. "She died of simple curiosity," said her doctor. "She had no serious ailment."

I, of course, as a practicing atheist (a credo I commend to no one), have no similar faith in a post-terrestrial future which I am certain does not exist, at least for me personally. I can therefore restrain my inquisitiveness. But I comprehend dear Maria's motive. I too realize I have become the survivor of a dwindled circle, a "last of the Mohicans" who helplessly detests the role.

So I take counsel from that gloomy dean, John Donne:

> Beza, a man as eminent and illustrious, in the full glory and Noone of learning, as others were in the dawning, and Morning, when any, the least sparkle was notorious, confesseth of himself, that only for the anguish of a Scurffe, which over-ranne his head, he had once drown'd himselfe from the Miller's bridge in Paris, if his Uncle by chance had not then come that way; I have often such a sickly inclination.
>
> And, whether it be, because I had my first breeding and conversation with men of supressed and afflicted Religion, accustomed to the despite of death, and hungry of an imagin'd Martyrdome; Or that the common Enemie find that doore worst locked against him in mee; Or that there bee a perplexitie and flexibility in the doctrine it selfe; Or because my Conscience ever assures me, that no rebellious grudging at God's gifts, nor other sinfull concurrence accompanies these thoughts in me, or that a brave scorn, or that a faint cowardlinesse beget it, whensoever any affliction assails me, mee thinks I have the keyes of my prison in mine owne hand, and no remedy presents it selfe so soone to my heart, as mine own sword.

Does one call it a reverie, a glum, lugubrious musing about past life and imminent death, as one ponders, seated upon a heap of brown pine needles gathered from beneath the whispering neighbors of my cypress perch rustling in the breeze? And how can such thoughts be wholly sad when interrupted by the baying of a little beagle rushing merrily through the underbrush, intent on a faded hare trail, the tip of his white stern occasionally peeping through the heather?

A dog is truly a man's best friend and gives him unquestioning love, devotion, and fidelity in exchange for companionship and food. Many of the leaders of our time trusted — and were trusted by — their dogs. Franklin Roosevelt's Falla was internationally famous. Richard Nixon's Checkers unwittingly participated in a scandal that almost terminated his master's career. Marshal Tito's Tiger, a large German shepherd captured from the Nazis, was the partisan leader's faithful companion for years after World War II, lying at his feet in its old age, listening to talk of state affairs while silently farting. General de Gaulle also had a large member of the same breed although, being a Frenchman, he called it an Alsatian and allowed it to sleep on his bed.

André Malraux, that fine and adventuring writer, entertained a fascinating theory. Mankind could be divided into two basic psychological groups: those who liked dogs and wood; and those who preferred cats and iron. By this he meant the tactile feel and sensuous smell of forested or carpentered or polished wood as compared with wrought iron or even steel. He would point out that his admired acquaintance, de Gaulle (the latter had only acquaintances, no friends — a remote, haughty man!) liked to spend his later days in retirement watching the woodsmen laboring among the trees of his gloomy forest retreat outside a northern French village.

I have never visited President Valéry Giscard d'Estaing in his office at the Elysée Palace when he was not accompanied by one of his weimaraners. During his latter days, Frederick the Great, a belligerent and schizoid Prussian ruler, spent most of his time lolling about with the only creatures who loved him — a pack of greyhounds.

Why do old men adore dogs and what inspires so many to take them along as would-be companions to the never-never land of death as I intend to do? My purpose is simple. There being no future, I cannot even remotely contemplate the happiness Christopher might give me in that "velvety cool blackness" foreseen by Winston Churchill. But I cannot bear the thought that he might be condemned to lead a forlorn, unhappy life, desperately seeking me day and night, when I, the only person who has loved him fully since Marina's death, have gone.

Old men do indeed adore dogs, sometimes because they are lonely and dogs are the best companions, and sometimes because the deceptions of a long life have embittered them and they seek the benevolence of a gay, pure partner with whom to share their age. Total solitude is scrupulously avoided by most people: it is an inhibiting state unnatural to humans, save for a handful of disciplined, eccentric saints. Thus, when such solitude is imposed on someone by life's immutable circumstances, a dog often becomes his constant accomplice and the confidant of his most secret thoughts.

I have traveled with dogs often in my life and Christopher, in my widowerhood, has been the greatest traveler of them all. Together we have discovered strange things about the human attitude toward canines. One of these, especially to be noted in Italy, Jugoslavia, and Greece, is that the farther I journey the more I become convinced that in the northern part of all lands (at least in the earth's upper hemisphere) the more people like dogs; and the farther south, the more the reverse becomes apparent. Why, I do not know, but I have always thought of death's geographic direction as being northward, and indeed the final sentence of my book on Brother Death concludes: "Now, old, old, old, with hair like thistledown, I sink with fatigue into the soft Aegean waters that bear me northward and backward into time." North I think of as a cold, anonymous direction — again, that "velvety cool blackness." It is south, with its vigor and passionate, heated fury, that means life — including its pleasures and its torments — inhabited by cagmag snudge, emotional humans, and thievish scaddle beasts.

My thoughts are interrupted by a slight spatter of rain. The sudden and frequently shifting Aegean wind whips a cloud across the sun and, to keep me company, there is a rustling of drops on the olive trees below. Christopher, intent on his busy explorations, seems to have discovered what anywhere else I might have taken to be a badger earth, not very recent. Yet to my knowledge badgers on Spetsais are even more rare than beagles — of which there is only one.

And just as the rain let up there must have been a shot. I could not hear it, being deaf in one ear anyway, but Christopher is aware of any noise — above all of a gun — far, far beyond the range of human detection and, never having been schooled to accustom himself to such devilish occurrences, was as is always the case, off like a streak of lightning. I knew it would be at least an hour, spent quivering in some secret hiding place known to him alone, before he would timidly creep back, his white-tipped tail dragging querulously behind.

I passed the time with my thoughts, watching the sun again emerge, and wondering why all Greek peasants are so intent on bird-murder, indeed the destruction of all animals. They fish at sea with dynamite, poisons, and nets, and even in the brawling trout streams of their heavily wooded northern mountain ranges they destroy the tiniest fish with nets or hand grenades. How sad to see them riding up the rough Spetsiot hillsides on a fine spring day, scatter guns strapped behind them on their wooden mule or donkey saddles, seeking the northward-bound and pitifully thin flocks of turtle doves migrating from Africa and Crete to upper Europe where each year fewer of them nest to produce fewer eggs and hatchlings because each year more of them are slaughtered on their traditional passage.

Some bees, attracted by the additional sweet scent excited by the momentary rain, were investigating the proliferation of early flowers, preparing to bring their honey back to their still winter-torpid queens. Greece has so much and such varied honey, I reflected, no wonder its gods were fond of mead, a drink now only known in Ethiopia and far from tastily brewed there. But where the Greeks live the bees dwell. In the Epirote forests near Albania there are honey trees, much coveted by bears. Along barren Mount Hymettus, outside Athens, the bees harvest each season's blossoms. And in that old Hellenic imperial state on the Black Sea, Trebizond (now Turkish Trabzon), an unusually dissipated race of bees manufactures from the flowers of the Pontic Azalea a honey so hypnotic and narcotic in its effect that it is legally forbidden to gather it.

Bees, like beagles, I reflected, and for that matter like all non-human creatures, have their own particular channels of communication and a special intellectuality which is wholly impenetrable to us who consider ourselves so superior as beings. Yet our tongues cannot distinguish between solutions of dissolved sugar and dissolved saccharine as can a bee, which will not touch the latter. Our ears cannot hear with anything like the acuteness of a beagle's ear and compared with a beagle's nose, my own is as useless as my appendix. It has been proven scientifically that his sense of smell is far more than a hundred times better than a human's. On Spetsais we have flowers requiring pollination which seem to emit odors like that of a female bee to attract the male. And the invisible radar system of the doves will send them flying in dozens from a set of trees at precisely the same instant although there is no hint of any danger nor any discernible signal by which they communicate with each other.

Dogs are blessed with some of these extra senses, including a remarkable memory for direction, smells, and people; and perceptiveness in terms of understanding humans — of knowing immediately who is their friend or enemy, being promptly aware of who fears them, and requiring at least as much friendship from mankind as mankind requires of them. Lyndon Johnson once told me, when meeting Christopher's predecessor, Benjamin Beagle: "You know, I have had many beagles but the one who knew me best was Little Beagle Johnson. He knew when I was unhappy and when I cried he would climb up on my pillow and lie beside me to comfort me." It was, admittedly, odd to think of this big, tough Texan weeping in bed next to a sympathetic little beagle. Myself, a curmudgeon, am no Willie the Weeper.

At this point Christopher again intruded in person on my thoughts, his twitching black moist nose emerging tentatively from a leafy bush, his eyes searching skeptically about for some putatively dangerous huntsman. A fair, tripping breeze was ruffling the sea below. The island was beginning to acquire a new freshness compounded of the light rain and the slowly descending path of the sun. Near the Peloponnesian coast across from us, the placid sea was still printed with the ephemeral pricks of raindrops, and great curtains of cloud hung low above the hills and plains behind the shore.

"Why do I like you best?" I asked him. "Is it because life, like most children, always saves the best for the last? Are you the icing on my dog cake, my puppy biscuit?" He examined me with those magnificent kohl-rimmed eyes, lovelier than those of any doe, clearly seeking to understand my question so that he might answer it and, failing, came closer with a slight whinnying noise, in order to have his chest scratched. As he did so his eyes caressed me with innocence, love, and abiding trust. You may think me unabashedly sentimental when I write about my small friend; that is what I am. Why restrain one's thoughts when one is about to do the foul, cruel deed of murder, albeit for a good and generous purpose?

I have had dogs almost all my life, fourteen in number, including noble representatives of many species among whom were two airedales, two wirehaired fox terriers, and two beagles. The last king of Afghanistan sent his royal kennelmaster to me in Kabul with ten magnificent purebred Afghan hounds (all, incidentally, visibly covered with ticks) to offer me my choice. Alas, I was forced to decline this regal largesse for I was on a globe-girdling tour during the old days of the propeller aircraft. I could not envision my newspaper happily paying extra fees for a magnificent animal standing over a yard high at the shoulder.

My very first memory is of a dog, Shandy, an airedale. Before any mental image of my mother or father, I can recall, at about two, sitting beside a vast light-brown and grey woolly creature that seemed to me then even larger than I knew a camel to be later. Fritz, another airedale, was stolen and evidently taken far away, but managed to make his path home a week later — filthy, bruised, and looking like an exhausted but deeply happy ragamuffin. Jeff, a small Boston bull-terrier, bit the nose of our cook whom he detested, and hung on until removed (with part of her nose) by the village fire department. (The cook poisoned him the next day. I loved Jeff.)

When I was twelve and sickly I used to spend some weeks each early summer at a modest Berkshire house owned by my former trained nurse, Miss Wilcox, all alone save for a large mongrel companion known only as "Hound." Hound and I fished trout and stickleback, roved fields picking berries, excavated caves in piles of damp sawdust at a lumber mill, raised a family of white rabbits which I taught him to respect, and trapped woodchucks with deadfalls and box-snares.

Fridtjof, a Great Dane I bought in Copenhagen as a puppy and smuggled aboard a ship on which I was working, only bit once in his tranquil life — a German police dog who constantly tormented him and stole his bones. One bite, and one German police dog dead of a broken neck; that was all.

Felix, a wirehaired, was won in a craps game where we were

all sitting on the floor rolling dice, glasses of champagne beside us. He was three months old. I accepted him in lieu of my winnings from a Polish diplomat because of his admirably eccentric taste for bubbly. I soon discovered the only other alcoholic drink he liked was Italian vermouth and soda. Every day at almost precisely six o'clock he demanded his drink, whining, scratching and making a nuisance of himself until he was served. Felix died, a war casualty, in Egypt as the drawn-out result of bomb wounds received in Greece.

It has always been obvious to me why Felix was killed. I had taken him in my arms to a Rome amphitheater where Mussolini was about to make a speech and where the press was accorded the honor of standing on the same dais as the duce. When he entered with a squadron of Blackshirts, right hand thrust forward in the Fascist salute, the huge crowd shouted *"duce, duce, viva, viva"* until he silenced them with both hands and began to speak. But Felix refused to keep quiet. He continued shouting *"duce, duce"* in a loud tonitruous bark echoed throughout by an intricate loudspeaker system until the crowd, being comprised of good Italians, burst into delighted laughter. Six *squadristi* rushed Felix and me right out of the place at top speed. And how does this relate to Felix's death? The raid in which he was struck by a bomb fragment as he lay on my bed is the only one in World War II in which an Italian bomber unit was led by Count Ciano, Mussolini's son-in-law. The target was clearly Felix, not the port and marshaling yards of Salonika. Imagine the duce ordering his daughter's husband: "Get that cur."

I cannot list all these dear friends but, looking back with sad nostalgia, I find I have reached the unchallengeable conclusion that beagles are best. The first of this splendid race to enter our family, Benjamin, deserves a special immortality as the only member of his race who preferred water to solid land. Marina wrote me from Spetsais when she first arrived with him from Paris in June, 1971, when he was an old dog of thirteen: "The boatman the other day could not believe his eyes because Beagle was swimming to the boat and the boatman gestured with his hands that the ladder was on the other side. So Beagle came to the other side and climbed the stairs all by himself and went to the towel, picked it up in his mouth, and dried himself. A genius."

He would swim anywhere in any water he could find and had to be chained on all boats bearing him, for otherwise he would jump overboard — from any height and at any distance from shore. Often he would go down to the sea himself and practice diving from a rock, barking, wagging his tail, leaping in, swimming back, again and again and again, with no need of an audience, but just for the fun of it. Even during the last summer of his life, when he was already fourteen years old, he could swim ten kilometers without once touching land.

Poor little Christopher, alas, has no such glamorous traits. Love alone marks his character. Agility marks his physique — he can turn at almost right angles while in midair during a gazelle-like leap. He likes all my friends and family, dislikes those I dislike. He has had very few close chums in his own world of dogdom with the outstanding exception of Papia, a large and handsome Irish setter (now dead) for whom he entertained immense admiration. I am certain he would rather be reincarnated as Papia (which means "duck" in Greek) than as Balto of Nome, Socrates, or Douglas MacArthur.

Christopher was born in Lincolnshire at the same kennel which produced Benjamin (with whom he shared four of their eight great-grandparents). He arrived in Paris, with me, at the age of three months. His pedigree name of Barvae Philip was promptly changed to Christopher because Marina and I believed a beagle was of a shape demanding a relatively long, thin name, three syllables being about right. A basset, so much longer, needs an extra syllable. The best basset name I ever encountered was Kilometer.

Christopher, even as a puppy, bore a remarkable facial resemblance to a Greek Orthodox saint, Saint Christopher Cynocephalus, of whom two portraits appear on icons in the Byzantine Museum in Athens and two others on icons in Moscow's Tretyakov Gallery. This likeness was rendered psychologically apt by that "bright and entirely misleading expression of innocence so characteristic of a beagle" as described by Thelma Gray in *The Family Beagle.*

Poetically I believe Christopher might be a reincarnation of his namesake whose descriptive name, Cynocephalus, means "dog head." The original claimant to that title lived in Antioch during the fourth or fifth century A.D. He was an unusually handsome man-about-town of good family and prosperous means, well acquainted with the agreeable things of life including wealth, wine, women, and song. There are various tales about how he acquired his unusual appearance. My favorite recounts that the good Lord became irritated with the young roué's vanities and pranks, leaned over the gold bar of Heaven, tapped him on the shoulder, and substituted a brand new canine head upon his neck. From that instant Christopher was spurned by his mistresses, banned from his usual clubs and restaurants, and eventually became a holy man because no other career remained open to him. In the end he died a martyr.

Cynocephalus was a product of the Near East's strong tradition of syncretism, fusing Christianity with one or more earlier pagan beliefs. It is thought by theologians that this special Saint Christopher derived in part from the dog-headed Egyptian deity and other sentimental baggage carried over from barbarians. The holy man of Antioch is first mentioned in theology's official literature in the tenth century and his earliest known portrait dates from the fifteenth. However, the intolerant iconomachy of the ninth century may well have destroyed many a pleasant image of Saint Christopher because it was especially harsh toward anthropomorphic art.

It is my conviction that dogs acquire the characteristics of their owners, rather than inherit traits from their parents or take after surrounding circumstances as Father Mendel and Chevalier de Lamarck respectively maintained. In support of this Labarkian theory I have discovered I can demonstrate what Christopher learned from me. For two years, from Marina whom he worshipped and who adored him, he acquired a charming gaiety and a preference for retiring late at night and curling up in sleep for hours in the morning. From me, over what alas became a much longer, lonely period during which he never forgot Marina and deliberately sought to comfort me, he acquired a perceptible tendency toward moodiness, an unusually loud voice (I am somewhat deaf) and a bark far deadlier than his bite, few friends (but much loyalty to them), a tendency toward nighttime insomnia, and greed. The esurient gusto with which Christopher devours his single daily meal is astounding. I am certain that if a bathtub were filled with hamburger meat he could eat his way out of it, leaving no speck behind and waddling away like a mini-hippopotamus.

My conversations with Christopher tend usually to be one-sided unless the subject is food in which case he proves to be a dog of action rather than of intellect. Our dialogues generally go like this:

Me: Do you promise not to run away if I let you off the leash? Even if you hear a shot?
C.: Yeow, yeow, yeeeow.

But on this, our last afternoon, I had brought with me one chapter of a book I never finished, and I said to him: "Now I am going to read you something aloud. So you must sit there and listen and pay attention."

He regarded me with an eager look and I began: "This is called 'Beagleophilia — A Treatise on the Best in Dogdom,' by me." He waited approvingly and I continued:

"Throughout history dogs have played a special and generally noble role. Perhaps the most famous early hound in literature was Argus, described in Homer's *Odyssey,* who when Odysseus, his master, returned after nineteen years from the Trojan War, lay almost paralysed, with dropping ears, yet still able to barely wag his tail. As the blind bard recounts: 'He had no sooner set eyes on Odysseus after those nineteen years than he succumbed to the black hand of Death.'

"In 'Locksley Hall,' Tennyson tells us that a dog 'hunts in his dreams,' and anyone who has ever watched a slumbering dog has seen him do it. Lord Byron's 'Inscription on the Monument of a Newfoundland Dog' reads: 'Near this spot are deposited the remains of one who possessed Beauty without Vanity, Strength without Insolence, Courage without Ferocity, and all the Virtues of Man without his Vices. This praise, which would be unmeaning flattery if inscribed over human ashes, is but a just tribute to the memory of Boatswain, a Dog.'

"Sir Walter Scott recounts in *Woodstock:* 'The eye of the yeoman and peasant sought in vain the tall form of old Sir Henry Lee of Ditchley as, wrapped in his laced cloak and with beard and whiskers duly composed, he moved slowly through the aisles, followed by the faithful mastiff or bloodhound which in old time had saved his master by his fidelity and which regularly followed him to church. Bevis, indeed, fell under the proverb which avers: "He is a good dog which goes to church for, bating an occasional temptation to warble along with the accord, he behaved himself as decorously as any of the congregation and returned as much edified, perhaps, as most of them." '

"Shakespeare, in *A Midsummer Night's Dream,* refers to hounds quite clearly much like Christopher: 'Their heads are hung with ears that sweep away the morning dew.' Nikos Kazantzakis talked of women with 'wet noses, like bitches,' who 'straight away smell out a man who desires them and one who doesn't.' Gaston de Foix wisely observed that 'a hounde will lerne as a man al that a man wil teche hym' and admired the way in which such animals would 'hunt al the day questyng and makyng gret melody in their langage and saying gret villeny and chydeng the beest that thei enchance.'

"In his *Traité de la Chasse* he instructed that his hounds must be allowed to run and play 'in a fair medow in the sun' and permitted to eat grass to heal themselves when sick. The gentle Frenchman confessed: 'I speak to my hounds as I would to a man . . . and they understand me and do as I wish better than any man of my household' — perhaps because he talked to them 'in the most beautiful and gracious language that he can.'

"Dogs have universally been admired by humans who sought their companionship. Takatoki, fourteenth-century regent of Japan, had such a passion for amiable canines that he accepted them in lieu of tax payments and kept up to five thousand dogs at a time in his gold-and-silver-decorated kennels, fed them boned fish and fowl, and had them borne upon palanquins when he wished them aired. Diogenes of Sinope, some twenty-five hundred years ago, was such a theriophile or animal lover, above all of dogs, that he lapped water as hounds did, sheltered in caves, and ate his food raw.

"Plutarch was the first to claim dogs had the faculty of reason and Montaigne insisted, 'their brutal stupidity surpasses all that our divine intelligence can do.' Ashley Montagu pointed out in his book, *Touching*, that the heart rate of many animals slows when they are caressed and 'it's an extremely rewarding and relaxing thing for an animal to be petted, which is why a dog will work for a pat almost as well as, or perhaps better than, it would for food.'

"Although early Christians — and many of their spiritual descendants — deny that beasts have immortal souls because, they argue, God created man in His image, most pagans (from Aesop to Buddha) deny such a false restriction. Indeed there is much evidence that dogs are and long have been widely associated with philosophy, with religion, and with death.

"The only other Christian dog-saint I have come across is Saint

Guinefort, a splendid French greyhound whose holy cult appears to have started some time after the eighth century and was first recorded by Etienne de Bourbon, a preacher-general of the Dominican order who died at Lyon in 1261. Guinefort belonged to the Lord of Villars in the Dombes. One day when the lord and his wife were absent from the family château, their baby son was attacked by a large serpent. Guinefort defended the infant but, during the battle, overturned the crib and spattered it with his own blood before killing the malefactor.

"When the infant's nurse appeared somewhat later and saw the bloodstained crib, upside down and containing no child, she thought the boy had been slaughtered by Guinefort. She ran to summon her master, and he promptly slew the hound with his sword. To his horror, shortly afterward, the unharmed baby was found near the snake's remains. Appalled at his deed, the Lord of Villars had his faithful dog buried near the château and planted the site with a ring of trees. For generations afterward peasants of the region visited the grave in the hope of curing sickly babies suspected of being changelings.

"The Dominican de Bourbon was disturbed by this superstition and had Guinefort disinterred. His vestigial relics as well as the trees still remaining were burned at the preacher-general's command but the cult persisted in the Lyonnais region and is known to have lasted at least into the early years of this century.

"The French have always had a greater weakness for dogs than the British, as far as I can discern. Even today they treat them as the equal of humans, serve them in restaurants (often ahead of their masters), allow them to sit beside the latter on aircraft and on occasion, if a dog is especially well behaved and has eyes like Christopher, serve him special delicacies. I am convinced that if Christopher is considered by divine powers to be exceptionally good when he dies, his soul will be parachuted to the Place de la Madeleine in Paris which contains not only his favorite restaurant, Lucas Carton, but also the most exquisite and well-stocked stores in the world for both known and little-known titillations of the palate.

"When France at last withdrew its veto of British membership in the European Community, I wrote a newspaper column praising the event and saying that now, as soon as the English learn to treat dogs as Europeans do, they would be effectively eligible members. But they have sold the world by their skillful propaganda that they, above all people, love dogs — although they quarantine them for six months before allowing them entry and yet, at the same time, never give them rabies injections, unlike all other Common Market members. It reminds me of the brilliant anti-Scottish propaganda begun by the court poet John Skelton in the sixteenth century which has led to the tradition that the Scots are stingy. It is my experience that they often look like drunken sailors when compared with their average southern neighbors.

"The French can boast that one Duke of Orléans had regular Catholic masses said for his dogs (despite theological claims of early Christians that dogs had no souls). The *messe des chiens* on Saint Hubert's day is a huntsman's custom that has dated from medieval times until today. That same aristocratic Duke Charles wrote poems to his spaniel with its drooping ears *(briquet aux pendantes oreilles)*. Spaniels were great favorites in France as well as in their original country, Spain, and Gaston de Foix described them as loving, loyal, and fond of coming 'before their maistre and playeng with their taile.'

"The Duke of Berry fed his small dogs on his own table and a medieval huntswoman considered it pleasant but not worthy of mention that greyhounds and spaniels slept on beds (as does Christopher). The old French dog-lovers disapproved of miniature-bred dogs — 'plafellows for minsing mistresses to beare in their bosoms to succour with sleep in bed.'

"Dogs have both personally and symbolically accompanied

their masters to death since time began. One finds their images painted (along with even more cats, the old Nilotics being distinctly feline although they had no iron to fondle, according to the Malraux theory) in many Egyptian tombs. Anubis was a dog-headed god, and Duamutef a dog-headed jackal for the polytheists of the most ancient nation state.

"The Chinese sculpted splendid dogs out of jade, and also relished them as food. Dogs were buried with Egyptian, Chinese, Greek, Hellenistic, and Viking masters in order to ease them in the upper or lower regions of the afterlife. And let us not forget Cerberus, the three-headed dog who guarded the gates of Hades.

"The crusaders often had their dogs buried beside them, as in the graves of London's Temple. Norse biers bore wolfhounds or elkhounds as well as stern axmen. And Strongbow, Earl of Pembroke, lies beside his little son (a mere child) — whom he slew for showing cowardice in battle — their dog stretched out beside them, in Dublin's Christ Church Cathedral.

"The great Duke of Berry, for whom that magnificent manuscript, the *Très Riches Heures* was designed and painted, personally visited a dog who refused to leave his master's grave, endowing a nearby peasant with sufficient money to keep the faithful animal well-fed for the rest of its life. The effigies of great, bold hounds were carven on the tombstones of their warlike lords, and those of lapdogs, often complete with collar and tiny bells, beside the memorials of their gracious ladies.

"It was widely recognized (in the words of a fourteenth-century writer) that a dog would always be 'wel folowing his maistre and doyng whatever he hym commandeth, he shuld be good and kyndly and clene, glad and joyful and playeng, wel willyng and goodly to all maner of folkes save to the wild beestis.' And thus, since man and dog first found each other, even before the art of fire-making was discovered, the latter has protected the former through what was thought to be eternity."

IV Christopher Beagle is a remarkable dog although he is perhaps not intellectually conscious of all the attributes which make him so. He is associated with world-renowned symbols. Charles Darwin made his most famous voyage of discovery aboard a ship named *Beagle*. There is a Beagle, Kansas; a Beagle, Ohio; a Beagle, Oregon; and a Beagle Bay, Australia; as well as a Beagle Island and a Beagle Channel, Chile.

The beagle is certainly one of the oldest hounds of the chase, hunting primarily by scent. Around 350 B.C. Xenophon surely was referring to beagles when he described hare-chasers in his essays, *Cynegeticos*. In A.D. 100, Arian, a historian, remarked that "they gladden so outrageously, even on a stale trail, that I have rated them for their excessive barking." (I have reproved Christopher for this, one of his more aggressive weaknesses.)

Oppian, another Greek writer who lived in the late second century of our era, described small hounds "giving tongue with a clanging howl." He added that he had discovered among the Britons:

> . . . a kind of dog of mighty fame
> For hunting, worthier of a fairer frame
> By painted Britons brave in war they're bred;
> Are beagles called, and to the chase are led.
> Their bodies small. . . .

Those "painted Britons" were undoubtedly the early, primitive Picts, and any well-versed English kennelmaster will assure you the beagle was brought to the "sceptered isle" by Rome's conquering legions. However, the French, whose chauvinism even has a canine branch, while admitting that beagles date back to Greek antiquity, insist their breed was improved by a much later infusion of Gallic blood and that they were introduced into the British islands by William the Conqueror. While acknowledging that a good beagle contains "a maximum of qualities in a minimum of volume" they resent the intrusion of English beagles now being reexported to France. They claim that acquired British blood threatens to destroy the best traits of the pure French dog because the immigrant's head is too much like that of a foxhound and menaces the delicate beauty of the distinguished Gallic line.

What is certain is that the beagle is far more popular in England than in France. (Christopher is proud of his island heritage.) There is considerable evidence that his ancestors roamed the English forests before the Norman hordes of William arrived, judging by descriptions of hunting dogs promulgated fifty years before the Battle of Hastings in *The Laws of the Forest of Canute*. These laws specially protected "long-eared" hounds, pronouncing them too small to harm the king's deer. What Duke William brought with him seems to have been the Talbot, which later became the southern hound and was perhaps crossed at a subsequent date with the proud little beagle.

The first Prince of Wales (later King Edward II) wrote to a friend in 1304: "I am sending some of our bow-legged harehounds of Wales who can discover a hare if they find it sleeping; and some of our running dogs who can swiftly chase it." Chaucer said of a lady dog lover: "Of smalle houndes hadde she, that she fedde. . . . But sore wept she, if one of them were dedde." The name "beagle" was well known by the time of Henry VII's reign. Dame Juliana Berners, abbess of a convent, who compiled the first known book on fly-fishing for trout around 1481, made laudable references to a little hound already known as a beagle although she referred to them as "Kennettys" and "Kenets."

King Henry VIII kept beagles. His daughter, the great Queen Elizabeth used them as hot-water bottles to warm her bed on chilly winter nights (a function they still perform effectively and with pleasure). King James I called his queen a "deare little beagle" and addressed his good friend the Earl of Salisbury as "my little beagill." A seventeenth-century zoologist wrote of "perriars or beagles, called in the German tongue Lochhundle" as "smelling dogs" and the modern author, Sir Arthur Bryant, says King Charles II hunted hares with beagles on Newmarket Heath. In one of John Dryden's seventeenth-century verses he speaks of a "graceful goddess . . . array'd in green, about her feet were little Beagles seen." Alexander Pope, a few years later, reported:

> To plain with well-bred Beagles we repair,
> And trace the mazes of the circling hare.

King William III, who died in 1830, kept a pack of beagles, as did King George IV. Sir Walter Scott warned lest "they rob us of name and pursue us with Beagles." The celebrated George Stubbs painted beagles; Queen Victoria tried to encourage a miniaturized breed. Even today "beagling" — afoot or on horseback — is a popular sport, especially in England, and as Thelma Gray informs us: "They will range about for a while until one gives a shrill cry, then the feathering of the sterns [tails] starts again and the merry Beagles are on the line once more. Away they stream in full cry. . . ." She adds with acumen:

A young Beagle will become very attached to its human family, and is capable of showing great affection toward the people it loves. Other breeds have this same habit but many carry it to excess, always yearning over somebody, jumping on their laps, screaming if shut in a room or car, never happy unless they are being fussed and petted. The Beagle, on the other hand, preserves its sturdy independence in any situation. It certainly enjoys a word of praise and a caress and will invariably grow into one of the most faithful of friends, but it is never likely to lose its inquisitive, questing nature and its liking for going about its own business occasionally.

I read this to Christopher who showed his displeasure. He finds that Thelma Gray knows too much about beagles and that this is disquieting. It was a page of one of her books which described his "misleading air of innocence" which he consequently destroyed. I consider her a genius.

Christopher, a well-traveled dog, prefers the life he knows on a Greek island and the fat life of Paris to any other existence with which he is yet acquainted. In Spetsais, he has a house in which he deigns to let other members of the family dwell although he considers every bed his own and occasionally ousts rival would-be occupants. As soon as the weather warms up in the early spring he becomes a passionate sunbather but always shows disappointment that despite all his efforts even the tan part of his tricolored coat becomes not one jot darker. He swims often (five times one January first) but never more than a minute or two at a time, displaying a fastidious little stroke at which his kinsman Benjamin would have sneered. Above the lapping waves his soft ears stand out like delicate shells listening with keen attention to the Aegean's multitudinous murmurs.

In a gustatorial sense he is astonishingly Greek. He adores white goat's cheese, grilled octopus, fried whitebait, and garbage in any and all forms but prefers it stinking and of Mediterranean origin. He has no sense of time (except lunchtime) and cannot distinguish between an hour and a week, which is also a Greek characteristic. Although he is little and looks even smaller and younger than he is, he believes himself to be another Hound of the Baskervilles and his bark would be admired by the Bull of Bashan. He ignores cats, disdains small dogs, and attacks large dogs, counting in a foolhardy way upon my protection. His preferred companions are human — and adults at that. Among them he dwells in unspeakable bliss, unspeakable, that is, except when he is "giving tongue."

When ordered to do anything he is highly disobedient, but perfectly disciplined on his own. He has a strongly developed sense of pride. When I go swimming — and I like to proceed considerable distances — he will wait an hour or more looking out to sea and sitting on my clothes to guard them; unless he feels I might require his aid and then he follows me along the shore-line, his eyes detecting me among waves even two hundred yards out. Although he has a catlike way of keeping himself clean, he is not obsessed by fastidiousness and, after one of his brief swims, adores rolling in the smelliest pile of filth he can discover. At such moments he feels boisterously grand.

In Paris, he has excellent restaurant manners and is always on good behavior when he is out on the town. He has often lunched at the British, American, Turkish, Cypriot, and Israeli embassies among others, weekended at the Rothschilds' and Clermont-Ton-nerres', and dined at the Castellanes' and Bordeaux-Groults'. He is the proud possessor of a diplomatic *laissez-passer* signed by the ambassador's wife (a great admirer) which reads: "This is to certify that Christopher Beagle is allowed to play in the British Embassy Residence garden whenever he wishes." It is stamped with the official embassy seal and signed by Ambassadress Mary Henderson.

Christopher's second-favorite restaurant, after Lucas-Carton, is La Fontaine de Gaillon, better known as Chez Pierre. In each of these he is always welcomed by the maître d'hôtel who will have had his usual meal of lightly grilled beef and carottes Vichy prepared in advance and served to him in a special plate laid out upon a linen napkin, a silver bowl of water beside it. Unlike Felix, he has no interest in wine or other alcoholic beverages. All day every day, before and after devouring it, he dreams of the single meal he is permitted. He eats faster than anything that ever lived and his plate never really requires washing because not a speck is left upon it.

He is a moody gentleman. In an instant he can shift from a deeply affectionate humor to indifference — and back. Sudden periods of pensiveness interrupt his frequent gay flights of mischief. On automobile trips — to which he is accustomed — he becomes passively but steadily carsick and never bothers to look out of the window, preferring to curl up sullenly on the floor. Yet he insists on never being omitted from even the shortest journey.

En route, although he hates car travel, the moment he is let off the leash in the countryside, whether it be a lush meadow in the Auvergne or a quiet white beach in Attica, he rushes back to his enemy the automobile because it is his traveling home, his moveable womb. He has a terror of open suitcases, always being convinced I am about to go away and leave him alone in his timeless eternity. When I return, after an absence of an hour, a day, a week or a month, I receive precisely the same joyous welcome of hopping squeals of delight, barks, and furious tail wags — or "feathering," as it is known in beagledom.

Physically, Christopher looks more delicate than he is, but he is very muscular and weighs nearly thirty-five pounds. He helps keep himself fit with a favorite yoga position, stretching at full length, his chest and forepaws on the ground, his rear paws stiffly erect and his stern pointed proudly heavenward.

His particular enemies come from the insect world. He is helpless before the assaults of ticks, fleas, and sandflies. Ticks diabolically seek out the crevices of his inner ear flaps and lodge themselves there growing overfed, green and swollen. I have pulled off some the size of hazelnuts and so groggy with his blood that it squirted inches when they were extricated from his tender skin. His reaction to this permanent state of war is a vigorous desire to attack all insects he discovers, from large ants to bees and horseflies, achieving painful defeats in these bouts as often as he gains a victory.

Christopher and I have become totally interdependent since Marina's death. Yet much as I admire him I confess that, regardless of his holy namesake, there is nothing even remotely sacred about his personality, despite the immeasurable humanity and understanding in his soft expression and peculiarly liquid eyes. When mesmerized by this tender gaze I have learned that it is best to be on guard against the unexpected, for it is precisely at such times that he's most likely to eat a brand new cashmere sweater, although in theory he has left puppyhood long behind.

It has now ceased drizzling. The mountain smells fresh and has become more acutely pleasurable: the scent of thyme, of tansy, of pine trees fragrant and pure. There is a rustling in the bushes — perhaps a restless turtle dove hiding there until evening before it resumes its predawn, boreal, migratory flight. Christopher's curiosity is promptly aroused.

He crawls amid the thorny twigs and stiff leaves, his progress only occasionally marked by the white feathering of his stern. If it is a bird it is a wily one; for nothing emerges except, eventually, a downcast beagle — followed two minutes later by a small Athena owl.

I take from the deep pocket of my bush jacket an anthropological book I thought proper to help guide my thoughts this final afternoon, Desmond Morris's *The Naked Ape.* It reads:

The most ancient symbiont in our history is undoubtedly the dog. We cannot be certain exactly when our ancestors first began to domesticate this valuable animal, but it appears to be at least ten thousand years ago. The story is a fascinating one. The wild, wolflike ancestors of the domestic dog must have been serious competitors with our hunting forebears. Both were cooperative pack-hunters of large prey and, at first, little love can have been lost between them.

But the wild dogs possessed certain special refinements that our own hunters lacked. They were particularly adept at herding and driving prey during hunting maneuvers and could carry this out at high speed. They also had more delicate senses of smell and hearing. If these attributes could be exploited in exchange for a share in the kill, then the bargain was a good one. Somehow — we do not know exactly how — this came about and an interspecific bond was forged. . . . Having been hand-reared, the dogs would consider themselves to be members of the naked-ape (human) pack and would cooperate instinctively with their adopted leaders. Selective breeding over a number of generations would soon weed out the trouble-makers and a new, improved stock of increasingly restrained and controllable domestic hunting dogs would arise.

Well, I must confess, regarding Christopher who has discovered a bone and is gnawing it ferociously beside the cypresses by Y Khara's chapel, like a jackal feeding among tombs, there is the descendant of that protracted symbiosis, the creature bound to me and me to him by an interspecific bond of love, but who shows no perceptible signs of being "increasingly restrained and controllable." Nevertheless, the setting is correct. "Joy."

TWO 🌿 The Education of Christopher Doghead

V

To reword Ovid, time, like a beagle, flies with noiseless foot, and we grow old. Both Christopher and I were stricken beyond grief by Marina's death and that was the start of time's true meaning. Her dearest wish in the hospital where she lay dying — unbeknownst to me, to herself, and above all to the doctors — was for me to try to smuggle Christopher into her room just so she could feel him, talk to him, play with him. But, when I confided this idea to a kind nurse she warned me against it, pointing out that no other patient nor any doctor could tolerate such a "germ-filled" transgression of the rules.

I sought consciously to set my mind to forgetting the awful tragedy of her abrupt end by drowning myself in work and constant travel. I rushed like a madman about the earth, seeing Jimmy Carter in Plains, Georgia and later in the White House and in Paris; seeing Colonel Qaddafi in a Libyan desert tent, seeing Egypt's President Sadat, Israel's Prime Minister Begin, the shah of Iran, the president of France, the German chancellor, and numerous other figures; writing, working, doing my best to drown out personal thoughts and heartfelt memories.

Yet soon I learned that not only is it untrue that the flesh and the devil can best be escaped by running away but precisely the same is the case with the spirit and an angel. And, as for the first part of the equation, if the devil in question is your very own self, the only escape is extinction. Christopher must have had similar thoughts. Whenever, on holiday in Greece, I oiled and cleaned my gun, he would moan lightly and watch me with sorrowful eyes.

More and more I realized that neither he nor I in any sense belong to the start of the new era — variously called technocratic or nuclear-missile by pretentious or sententious posturers — but that we represent the very finish of an old era which everyone said had ended with the start of World War I but which in fact is loitering on to the preliminary bouts of World War III. Maelstroms would sweep away most of mankind and beaglekind and, whatever happened, there would be little old and an enormous amount of new about it. But I knew and Christopher seemed to know that this was not to be for us; we were already on what might be called the "safe" side of that frontier. My gout became worse and he developed rheumatism. I calculated and found that if I lived to be seventy-five years old, which now seems to be the normal span, he would then be fourteen, the normal span for his happier, more intense species. Yet, somehow I increasingly felt that we would not go so far along the path; that both of us would quit it earlier, side by side.

Such unpleasant but realistic and certainly not mournful thoughts disturbed both of us once they became plainly manifest. I will venture to say that this was when the newspaper which had employed me for almost thirty-eight years and which, under previous managements, had honored and respected me, stabled me in what was called "mandatory retirement" for reasons of age although several older colleagues were not so affected. Suddenly I realized that the primordial daily task of what life remained to me was the education of my dog-headed, human-souled friend, Christopher Beagle.

Christopher was already a moderately well-known Paris boulevardier but by preference he was by no means as eager a world traveler as, for example, my wartime companion Felix, the hard-drinking fox terrier who enjoyed wandering the globe for its own sake. Felix adored airplanes, trains, and automobiles. Christopher was more sedentary by nature. But he also liked going out, participating in social events.

When I began my initial feckless week of unemployment in January, 1978 — the first since I was twenty-one years old — I also began the deliberate education of my dog-headed friend. He was already four years old, a slow starter; for Marina and I had been so fascinated by his frolicsome, unpredictable, mischievous personality that we had neglected his cultural development. Unlike Benjamin Beagle, his predecessor, he never even learned to beg — the simplest of all tricks for greedy dogs. Nor was he much of a swimmer. During four holidays, to a chorus of mockery from my children, grandchildren, and their friends, I had given him swimming lessons: the old-fashioned type, attaching a chain to his collar and patiently walking up and down near the shore in about two feet of water, so he simply had to keep himself afloat by his own efforts. He does swim now, all on his own and by his personal preference, but he is not very good at it.

Since, in my newly straitened circumstances — living on a fixed pension amidst a period of roaring inflation and economic depression — I could no longer take Christopher to his favorite restaurants to lunch on steak and carottes Vichy, I brought him along on almost every occasion when I was invited to a friend's house for a meal. Being quite as extroverted as Marina had been, he relished this with gusto.

On January 14, 1978 he devoured foie gras as it is prepared in the homeland of our host, Ambassador Jean-Marie Soutou, the highest-ranking official and secretary-general in the French Foreign Ministry, while Maribel Soutou and Nicko (the British ambassador) and Mary Henderson watched with affectionate admiration. I fear he was less interested in Jean-Marie's observation that the definite majority of French people are pro-American and only the Communists and Gaullists anti, than he was in the liver.

Princess Olga of Greece and Denmark, widow of Prince Paul of Jugoslavia, and an old friend, invited Christopher and me for tea soon afterward: a beautiful woman, then seventy-eight but tall and straight with a good figure, lovely features, and a pleasant voice. Talking with her was always like visiting another era. She was of Romanov descent on both sides and insisted on lending me a book of photographs of the Russian aristocracy and loyal old illiterate peasants. She patted Christopher, gave him a cookie which he ate out of politeness (he doesn't care for sweets) and asked if I "felt" Marina with me much of the time. "All the time," I said. "It's both depressing and sustaining."

"Ah," she sighed. "It's just that way for me with Paul."

I am an atheist, as she knew, but she was reading a book of mine called *Go Gentle into the Night*, a few pages every evening, and couldn't really believe I had no faith in a god. She herself was certain of some form of "continuity" or afterlife and was in touch with the late prince, she told me, through a medium who assured her he was immensely happy and that the former Jugoslav regent, a cultivated aesthete, "was astounded at the beautiful music he heard." She added: "It is hard for me to explain these things to others. But you understand. My husband is always with me, as Marina is with you."

One day American ambassador Arthur Hartman came for lunch. Only subsequently did he acquire a beagle bitch named Abigail to whom Christopher is officially affianced. Art talked of his ambassadorial embarrassments during President Carter's recent visit to Giscard. The U.S. guest had insisted that his French host's very grand dinner at Versailles (which I attended) should see the ladies wearing long dresses; but the men in business suits. Likewise, Giscard sent word to Carter that if he wished to see the opposition chief, Socialist Francois Mitterrand, he couldn't go to the latter's office but only receive him at the embassy, which was legally U.S. "territory." Finally, he strongly discountenanced Carter's visit to the town hall where the Gaullist Jacques Chirac, Giscard's theoretical partner in the majority but a man he hated, was mayor of Paris.

Our farewell Parisian meal was lunch at my apartment with the Soutous and Diane de Castellane, who had brought her little bitch Lily, an old friend of Christopher's. Jean-Marie said that the first foreign ambassador in Paris to call upon him and congratulate him on the French government's electoral victory had been the ambassador of Poland. The Pole told Soutou that Polish policy is based on two foundations — Russia and a stable France. He added that France would not have been stable had the left won.

The time had come to prepare for our long journey by car to Spetsais. Christopher enjoyed his Paris routine of a six-mile walk each day, a hearty lunch, a nap, and occasional sorties to visit friends. But the moment the empty suitcases appeared — including his own carrier, which contains a mixture of canned dog food, puppy biscuits, his plate and bowl (for hostile caninophobe countries like Greece and Jugoslavia), plus an assortment of towels and toys — he knew that travel impended. He didn't like the concept; and yet he would do anything to avoid being left behind. He stressed this by getting into each successive suitcase until it was filled up and closed. Only after the car had been loaded and Jovita, our sweet little cook who would fly down to open the house in Greece after locking up in Paris, had waved farewell and the doors were slammed, did Christopher relax and curl up on the floor before the front seat like a soft, barely animate pretzel.

We drove together on a splendid, sunlit day through the Auvergne — a marvelously beautiful French province not yet overrun and overdeveloped — with rolling green hills, forests, pastures filled with flowers, and everything dominated by the great mountain range, le massif Central, still covered with gleaming white snow.

There are many trout streams in the area and we spent our first night at a tiny modest inn on the bank of one of these, called l'Allagnon, that went rushing by almost beneath us. On the front porch of the *auberge* was a sign issued by the government detailing the differences between the local *truitelle*, a midget brown trout, and the *tacon*, a midget Loire salmon. It is legal to keep the *truitelle,* no matter how small; but the *tacon* must be released to swim eventually downstream, along the Loire River and out into the Atlantic whence it returns years later and full-grown, to spawn and die. Christopher was less interested in these piscine distinctions than in two Auvergnat cheeses, Fourme d'Ambert and St. Nectaire, the first from sheep's milk, the second from cows', both of which he adored and gobbled up. He has a passion for cheese.

Next morning, after Christopher had an early swim, gamboling about in the current, we took off again, traveling through the Lot valley and visiting the large cathedral at Rodez. After a hasty inspection, and seeing no one around the cathedral square or within it, I took Christopher inside. He is fond of churches; not only are they pleasantly cool but they appear to be filled with fascinating aromas.

From there we drove on to Albi, whose immense cathedral I adore, and a very kindly friar invited me to bring Christopher in with me — a visit which was regarded with much distaste by a party of sightseeing tourists. The friar smiled gently and told me to pay no attention. He was a Franciscan, of course, and like the founder of his order adored all living creatures.

Albi was the center of a powerful medieval heresy. A church council was called in its diocese in 1165 and the heretics, known as Albigensians, were publicly condemned. I tried to explain to Christopher that this lovely area had run with rutilant rivers of blood because of the Catholic employment of hard-boiled loyalist mercenaries who squashed Albigensians, Arians, Cathars, Gnostics, Manicheans, and Waldensians as dissenters. Christopher looked at me without interest. It seemed from his expression that he was remembering the taste of Fourme d'Ambert.

We spent the night at a horrid beach resort called Valras Plage which looks like the ghastly Bulgarian playground erected by Soviet planners along the Black Sea coast. At the mere sight of it Christopher ran away, two miles down the sand, almost getting himself killed by heedless drivers gunning beside the dunes.

The following day, we visited yet another church, that of Saint Nazaire in Béziers. It had been destroyed in 1209 by one of the antiheretic leaders, Simon de Montfort, but was subsequently rebuilt with one facade boastfully showing a triumphant Catholic church and a defeated Jewish synagogue. I explained to Christopher that Albigensians were not Jews; simply the ancestors of today's southern French Protestants.

He reflected silently on this as we drove through Montpellier to the fortified harbor of Aigues-Mortes from which Saint Louis, king of France, sailed for his Seventh and Eighth Crusades against Egypt and Tunis. In Tarascon on the Rhône, which contains a storybook castle, I took my small friend to yet another church where he was again welcomed by an amiable priest. Then, when we entered the weird, flat, bird-filled jungle of the Camargues, I encouraged him to roam about after devouring his tin of luncheon. This time, instead of retreating to his automobile, he discovered a herd of ponies and amused himself greatly by barking and chasing them into the thickets.

We spent the night near the bauxite mining center of Brignoles at a charming country inn called Lou Paradou ("paradise" in the Provençal dialect), once again on a trout stream, named the Caramy. As the sun began to set, several fine fish rose and Christopher chased them, splashing and occasionally swimming with exuberant enthusiasm but no angler's success. In the morning we drove to the twelfth-century Cistercian abbey and church of Le Thoronet, high and spacious, built of pink and yellowish limestone and set in a glade amid forested, bird-filled slopes. Hence, we proceeded to Le Castellet, an old Phoenician village near Toulon, where our good friends Sir William and Lady Deakin live.

Pussy is Rumanian by birth and Bill, as a wartime parachutist, headed the first British mission dropped in to Marshal Tito and his partisans in the mountains of southern Jugoslavia: a small, exceedingly intelligent man who earned a great reputation for his bravery. They had just come back from a stay in a Jugoslav state-owned castle in Slovenia where they were Tito's guests. They spent the marshal's birthday with him at a party and Bill found he was in quite good health, despite his great age (eighty-six), his obviously red-tinted hair, and his massive overweight.

Christopher and I slept on a broad bed in the room above Bill's working quarter, set apart from the house itself. After breakfast we took a fine walk down from the hilltop, where there is a medieval fortification erected on the site of an earlier Roman fortress. While Christopher whizzed off, nose down, tail up and wagging (forgive me, stern feathering), Bill talked more about Jugoslavia.

Tito had been sent there secretly in the 1930s and then, after returning to Moscow, was ordered back again in 1940. He traveled by boat from Odessa to Istanbul with a Croat named Kopinić and they picked up a Greek Communist girl in Turkey, who later married Kopinić. Tito was traveling with a forged Canadian passport but he suspected the Comintern of giving away agents it distrusted by issuing them with bum documents. So he obtained a Greek passport under the name Spyridon Tikhon. But when he tried to get a Jugoslav visa at the consulate in Istanbul, the consul was suspicious because he didn't speak Greek. So, instead, Tito bought a ticket on the Italian steamer *Conte di Savoia* from Genoa to the United States and then, with the ticket, was able to obtain a transit visa from the Jugoslavs. In Zagreb he went underground. Moscow, already trying to split the Jugoslav party in 1940, instructed Kopinić to form his own "loyal" organization.

Christopher was less interested in all this than in the fact that he had discovered and killed a fat little field mouse which he produced with the pride of a mighty hunter. Our last evening was spent chatting over bottles of wine on the terrace looking down toward the Mediterranean. Next day we left for Italy.

Mindful of the fact that the Italians were in a great state of jitters because of the wave of terrorism bursting over their country, I had obtained in Paris a letter from Rome's envoy requesting the authorities to be cooperative with me and calling to their attention that my shotgun was only for hunting and that my dog was also coming along. These precautions proved entirely counterproductive.

Rather than the usual crossing, I was sent on to a second frontier post where the carabinieri chief telephoned Imperia to get instructions. Then carefully he read, not once but three times, a whole series of folders dealing with the eventuality of transiting a shotgun. He then typed out a report (with one finger). He was barely literate and a blithering fool to boot. The whole process took almost two hours. The only thing I could do while he dawdled was walk Christopher (who was dying of thirst, and they had no water) and examine the dozens of photos of Red Brigade members posted on the walls as "wanted."

Fortunately we found a pleasant hotel on the sea in Imperia and had a long agreeable walk on a wharf extending far out over the water. We dined on *seppioline* which turned out to be the same as Greek *calimarachia* (squids), but not as good, looking like bloated spiders.

In Senigallia, on Italy's Adriatic coast, I noted: "About the only thing I can find that this town is famous for is that it was the birthplace of Pope Pius IX. Thus, papal infallibility began here, one might say. The only other infallible thing about the place seems to be the rain: all the time since Christopher and I arrived. It's a hideous coast, flat and dreary.

"We drove from Arezzo via Urbino, across lovely mountain country with woods, clouds, and rivulets. But Arezzo, which Marina and I used to love twenty-odd years ago, has become a dump. Indeed, all of Italy except the Apennine region is overcrowded with jerrybuilt factories and flimsy, hideous apartments in the best Czechoslovakian architectural style. When we finally arrived here, tired and dusty, they said they'd take the dog and then when we had unloaded all of the luggage and put the car in a parking space, they blithely informed me Christopher would not be allowed in the restaurant. 'Either we both go in — or we both leave,' I said. There being very few customers, they gave in. Christopher likes it here better than I, even sometimes frolicking on the beach despite the rain, which he detests."

Arezzo is an ancient Etruscan town and for a long time in the Middle Ages contested Florence in Tuscany — until it was dominated in 1348. It has some fine churches in the old city containing paintings by Luca Signorelli and Piero della Francesca. Petrarch was born there.

It was much harder for modern man to destroy Urbino, birthplace of Raphael, because the old town surrounded by walls is situated on a steep hill in a beautiful mountain location. It was ruled by the famous Montefeltro family from the twelfth through the fifteenth century. There are several Pieros and Signorellis there, and the ducal palace is a Renaissance masterpiece.

I can not help but feel that the central problem with Italy is its lazy, stupid bureaucracy. Most private citizens I have come across have been friendly and courteous but the government-paid functionaries are almost uniformly morons — disobliging and only eager to watch the clock. This goes for the reputed carabinieri too, at least those I have encountered, and it makes the exploits of terrorists like the Red Brigade far more easily comprehensible. Fascism stuffed the bureaucracy with loyal dolts, as communism did in Russia, and too many of their like remain. I noted:

"Drove from Senigallia to Bari. Ancona, the first city we passed, was founded around 400 B.C. by the Syracusans, themselves a Greek colony. So it was the colony of a colony. It was a favorite resting place of Trajan.

"Further down the coast is the tiny town of Loreto which boasts that it contains the House of the Virgin Mary, transported there by angels in 1291 and then removed by them a second time (from a place near Fiume, its first resting place) in 1294 to a laurel wood from which Loreto takes its name. Bramante was among those who later completed the sanctuary of the holy house, which also includes frescoes by Melozzo da Forli and Luca Signorelli.

"Whizzed by Pescara, a relatively modern and shabby resort town, remembering a long conversation I had with Pope Pius XII more than a quarter century ago in which all he could discuss, in this complex world, was the probable outcome of a local election in Pescara and its effect on the Italian political picture. He was up to the elbows in politics.

"From Bari down, there are still many *trulli,* round huts of whitewashed stone, without mortar and with conical roofs of the same material, looking like large gothic igloos. They seem to have been in these parts since time began — even in Brindisi, one of Rome's important naval bases in ancient days.

"Several things strike me after this tour of Italy. I am astounded by the frequent corruption at all levels. I am impressed by the fact that, like all Europe, Italy is being speedily and frantically covered by monstrous towns and villages. Yet I am equally impressed that hidden away in even the largest concentrations of ugliness are incredible treasures — paintings, cathedrals, castles.

"Finally, I am amazed by the total absence of American automobiles. Some years ago they were coveted, useful, status symbols. But U.S. manufacturers are so blind that they have lost the export market with overgrown dinosaurs that use up too much steel and chromium and consume far more gas than foreign cars (which are also prettier). Last Sunday I checked about five thousand cars parked in or creeping through Senigallia. I listed: English — Austin, Rover, Ford Granada (made in the U.K.); French — Peugeot, Renault, Citroën; German — Volkswagen, Opel, Audi, Mercedes, Ford Taunus (German made), BMW; Italian — Fiat, Alfa Romeo, Lancia; Swedish — Volvo; Japanese — Honda. The only American cars I saw were one beach buggy and one Chevrolet (with Swiss plates).

"I think cars are beginning to resemble humans in my benighted country. We breed bigger and bigger Americans who think less and eat more. (Cars just drink more.)"

I was struck by the impression that the further south you go in Italy the poorer the people are; and the worse the hotels and restaurants become, the more they dislike dogs. Christopher discovered this to his woeful regret. We were turned away by one after another hotel and restaurant because of him.

At the Torre Cintola vacation-village hotel, an imitation Club Méditerranée project where we stayed outside Monopoli, a big, strong, young man sitting beside me at my table moved away when he saw Christopher lying small and peaceful underneath. A young woman got up and left when she discovered Christopher eating daintily beneath the table. South Europe is not dog-loving. Maybe that's what's wrong with it. It has been conquered repeatedly during history and is notoriously corrupt.

All Brindisi authorities — and they are endless — predicted unctuously that I wouldn't get Christopher on the *Egnatia*, a Greek boat. He hadn't the least bit of trouble.

VI   Greece again! The boat stopped first at Corfu in the early morning, gleaming and lovely. We chugged on to Igoumenitsa where there was a scramble for gasoline coupons (cheaper against hard currency). Then off toward Janina and Metsovo. The last time I was in the Pindus was during the autumn-winter-spring of 1940 to 1941 when the Greeks thrust back an Italian attack but at last were overwhelmed by a German offensive in April, 1941. In those days it was tough, cold country. The roads were terrible — rutted dirt paths broken apart by jams of military transport, outmoded trucks, and plenty of horse-and-mule-drawn vehicles. Now there is a good road as far as Janina, along the Aöös River, and on to Metsovo. Up and down we went through the ancient ranges, patches of snow still gleaming in the upper valleys shaded by peaks. There are great forests and many little streams; not at all like arid Attica.

Janina has grown considerably and is no longer the pleasantly dilapidated Balkan town through which cavalry officers trotted four decades ago. But it still looks tranquil, with the large, unruffled green lake where Ali Pasha, the Epirote tyrant of the early 1800s, used to drown his wives in sacks filled with sugar to make death sweet, and where he entertained Lord Byron.

Arrived in Metsovo at lunchtime and drove to a simple restaurant which served Christopher three steaks, at my insistence, and me one. I think Christopher likes me because I follow the old formula that an officer provides for his men before he provides for himself, although I have never been an officer and Christopher has never been a man. But the theory is sound, he believes.

When we returned from lunch, Mrs. Yanni Averof, wife of the mayor (who is a nephew of my old friend Evanghelos Averof, minister of defense), came by the hotel for coffee. She insisted I move to the guest house they have established in the museum created by the Averof Foundation, which Evanghelos founded and which she heads. She is a charming, pretty young woman with three small children. The six-year-old boy and two-year-old girl became so enamored of Christopher that the latter cried when he left after she first met him.

We strolled through the village, which has a population varying between two thousand, in wintertime, when the shepherds move their flocks to the plains of Thessaly, and three thousand in the summer. It is delightfully old-fashioned and colorful with many stone houses covered by thick slate roofs, the slates being carefully laid on without any mortar or any discernible pattern. The foundation is trying to keep Metsovo nontouristy, encouraging the population to do more and better what they know how to do — excellent weaving of local wool, with patterns of vegeta-

ble dyes; manufacture of smoked cheese and of a new local parmesan; the start of a wine industry with cuttings from the Bordeaux region; and specialized woodworking. Metsovo now has a
monopoly on the kegs in which feta cheese is kept throughout
Greece.

Christopher and I walked all over. Most people wear old-fashioned woven wool costumes like they did at the time of the
Revolution, more than one hundred and fifty years ago —
the men in black with small hats and baggy bloomers; the women
in heavy, long, patterned skirts and shawls over their heads. We
passed the sawmill with its lovely smell of freshly cut wood.
Evanghelos Averof personally saw to it, after World War II, that
the entire region was reforested — with impressive results. The
rapid land erosion ended, a modest system of flood control was
established in the river below, and there was a renewed source
of raw material for the woodcarving and timber industry.

The majority of the Metsoviti are Vlachs — nomadic tribes
of Rumanian-speaking shepherds. They have been wandering
around these parts since the days of Roman garrisons, from Dacia
(Rumania) down to Thrace and Albania. Yanni Averof believes
that Vlachs are concentrated along the old Roman imperial high-
ways and are descended from troops who married local people.
Most live in Metsovo and tend their flocks from here, go off in
the cold weather to return only in spring. They speak Vlach
(from the Rumanian province of Wallachia) at home and some
don't even know Greek.

Yanni is a fine, energetic man. Elena was born in Rumania, of
a Rumanian-Greek family, and left only fifteen years ago. She
met and married him later. They speak English with the children. Their life is good, simple, unpretentious. Elena does the
cooking and we dined in the kitchen. Their house is filled with
the local weavings she is seeking to encourage as a cottage industry.

Metsovo is an oddly pleasant historical throwback, achieving

what Gandhi, on an immense scale, sought for India: home indus-
tries and faithfulness to high-quality local products. The village
had sheltered a refugee Turkish nobleman in the seventeenth
century so, when he left, he obtained for it a favored position
under the sultans. Many prosperous refugees came here as a
result. Two families dominated events: the Averofs and the
Tositsas. George Averof made a large fortune in the Odessa grain
trade. When he died he left many endowments to the village and
bequeathed a large sum to Athens with which the government
bought a battleship, although he had enjoined the legacy should
be used for "peaceful purposes." Evanghelos, my friend, adopted
the name Averof-Tositsa because the last Baron Tositsa was
childless and requested the link of names and heritages in exchange for aiding the village.

Coming back from the sawmill I heard a pleasant noise of
music and stopped to watch a crowd of men dancing the *sirto*
round and round by a taverna while musicians played, and people sang and drank wine.

The village possesses a curious local phenomenon: twenty-
eight "arrow pigeons." These originally come from Thessaly.
They are trained by experts to circle high, high up in the sky and
then shoot down like bullets, wings folded tight, until almost
striking the earth, at which point they open their wings and glide
away. There are competitions and the winner is the bird who
comes closest to hitting the ground. Some occasionally misjudge
and are killed.

Elena Averof took us to the museum — a reconstructed version of the old stone house of the Tositsa clan, which boasted the
title "Baron."

The house was a wreck after the war and civil war but Doxia-
dis, the famous architect and city planner, took charge of its
reconstruction in the late 1950s and King Paul and Queen
Frederika came for the grand opening, dressed in local traditional peasant costumes.

The Tositsa house and that of the Averofs, where Yanni and Elena live, were the two grand places of Metsovo. They are almost fortresses, built of blocks of limestone with narrow small windows on the lower floors to make defense against attack easier, for the surrounding mountain region was thick with klephts (armed bandits) and there were also occasional forays by the Turks.

The front door opens onto a large internal courtyard where the horses were led in and next to which was a fully equipped internal stable. These houses were so designed that the inhabitants and their retainers could withstand a siege of several months, fully equipped with food, olive oil, wine, water (from internal wells), arms, ammunition, etc. The stable is adorned with beautifully embroidered saddles almost two centuries old. By the horses' stalls are posts on which are hung cowbells, each with a different sound so each animal can be recognized at a distance.

Only the grandee families had internal toilets and running water. The idea was that the house could be closed up tight against a hostile world, when need be. There was always the threat of kidnapping by klephts. The lower floors have a large kitchen, huge wine barrels, stacked firewood.

When strangers came to Metsovo all, including Turks, were expected to descend from their horses and wipe their feet before entering the village, shaking off the dust of the subjected land outside; Metsovo had a special quasi-independent status.

The museum features a collection of magnificently ornamented guns, pistols, blunderbusses, and swords with silver scabbards from the famous silversmiths of Janina. Upstairs is a "summer room" where the leading family members could keep cool, lying along narrow Turkish-style wall divans and with windows facing away from the afternoon sun; and a "winter room" with no windows, a fine fireplace, and two enormous low beds where many people slept side by side, packed like sardines — partly for warmth. Here and there are dowry chests from the Orient which were used by family brides.

Local costumes have been collected in wall closets. The seigneurs wore white cloth; the rest black. Men wore shoes with pom-poms, like the evzone dress uniform; women wore sandals with high toes and heels of wood to keep clear of mud. They had beautiful gold and silver embroidered dresses.

The kitchen holds a big oven, a stove, a big churn, many mortars and pestles, a flour bin, and other utensils. In the bedroom of the family head is a small balcony where gypsy musicians sat and played (out of the way, allegedly, because they smelled so bad). A wonderful collection of icons has been put together on the walls. Saint George of Janina is featured, being flayed alive by the Turks.

After the museum, where we were accompanied by Christopher and two of the Averofs' children, Elena and I went down a steep slope beyond the village to see its famous twelfth-to-thirteenth-century church and monastery which Vangheli Averof actually discovered beneath the dung and smoke-blacked walls of a stable. Outside is a little porch where crazy people were chained up all night on each January 6, name day of the church's patron saint, Nicholas, because he was the protector of the insane. If they survived the cold, they were freed. Most froze to death.

Inside, there are beautiful frescoes which have been painstakingly cleaned — the entire inside of the small church, including its barrel vault, is wholly covered with paintings. Over the entry door is a very rare icon of the Virgin Mary giving her breast to the Christ child.

The church was initially restored in the seventeenth century by three klephts who wished to save their souls after an evil life. A small section is barred off and invisible in the rear where women were isolated, as in a harem, on the special occasions when they were allowed in church at all.

Yanni, Elena, Christopher, and I lunched on souvlakia and lots of drink in the village square with a large group of Metsoviti, all men, drinking *tsipuro* (the local marc) and beer. In the afternoon Yanni took us fishing together with three other local enthusiasts, among them a young Vlach who had been sent to Italy to learn how to make provolone and parmesan cheese and now runs the local cheese factory.

We fished a tributary of the Arakhthos River, scattering flocks of wild pigeons and turtle doves. It was lovely but the water was warm and the fish few. One man used a big spinning rod. Another used throw-nets and thus trapped three small ones.

Supped at the Averofs' and discovered I had known Elena's father, Nicky Chrissavaloni, a dashing Rumanian-Greek banker, in Bucharest between 1939 and 1941. He came to Athens in 1961 with his family and died a decade later. His family originated in Chios, where part of Marina's came from. An ancestor fled the famous Turkish massacre by swimming, was picked up by a British boat and dropped off at Rumania. The captain gave him a single gold piece for luck. With this he built his fortune.

Next day, Elena and the children left early for their summer house on the island of Skiathos so Yanni took the day off and showed me around. We went to the wine factory, then the park given by the philanthropic old George Averof at the place where he bade his mother farewell before going off to make his fortune in Russia. He promised to come back and make a park there if he succeeded. It is lovely, tree-filled, and peaceful, and includes a deer enclosure. All but two were killed by wolves who broke over the fence last winter. Then we went to the cheese factory where Christopher was enchanted by the smells.

In the afternoon we piled into a large, efficient Rumanian-made Land Rover and drove across Greece's highest plateau among the Pindus peaks, finally descending horrible rutted paths through silent tall forests to a tributary of the Aóös River, where we fished with very little success. Only those who used crude throw-nets or two-man scoop nets got a few tiny trout. But it was the loveliest river I've ever seen, blue-green and flowing through a silent pine forest — not even birds around to disturb the total tranquility and the slight purling of the flow. Got home late so took Christopher for souvlakia in the main square.

Met Yanni at the church Sunday. Women were coming out one entrance, buying candles for their saints. Men came out another entrance and filed through a little park. Because it was the fortieth day after a villager's death, according to custom trays of grain and sugar were dipped into by hand and munched. Although the women had on colorful long dresses and shawls over their heads on which were pinned fake gold coins and from which hung braided pigtails, also usually fake, almost all the men wore their best modern "store suits." There were a few in the traditional black coat or kilt and black or white tight leggings, black pom-pom shoes and black round skull caps; but they were all very old. They have one bench in the park where each of them is entitled to his regular seat, like a London club. They sit and gossip. Sometimes, when the movie house functions in wintertime, they go to a film together — especially if it is somewhat pornographic.

A local boy was marrying a Patras girl. Weddings are always held on Sundays. Two days previously the girl's dowry — all the embroidery, curtains, sheets, towels she has been preparing since childhood, plus furniture for their new house (not money) — had been paraded through the streets. The ceremony started off with a gypsy orchestra (from the special gypsy quarter of the village — gypsies are still socially looked down on as "black") strutting through town and up to the bridegroom's house, playing noisily all the way. They initially comprised a lutist, a violinist, a clarinetist, and a drummer. A second violinist joined later. They stayed at the groom's house, drinking and playing while the drum was garlanded with roses.

Yanni and I then walked to the café off the main square with

Christopher, now hailed as "Christoflai" by all the village children, who adore him. We sat under a shade tree drinking *tsipuro*. At another table were some of the old men with their pillbox hats and shepherd's crooks, solemnly regarding the cars arriving for the wedding. One man at our table fingered a *kombeloi* (worry beads) of dice. It was an agreeably peaceful setting.

Yanni later took us across a small river to the neighboring village, called Anhelio (without sun) because in the winter the limited sun is cut off by the high peaks. It was quite fascinating: the "president" of the little village (population, 1,000); a fine-looking Vlach shepherd of fifty-five with weathered features; a carpenter; the restaurant owner (it was just four little tables in the village general store); and his wife, who was surely once very pretty, with blond hair, blue eyes, a broad, smiling mouth. Most Socratic. The shepherd — who trucks his sheep to Thessaly each winter for the lower pastures — wondered why men have so many languages when they are otherwise so much alike. He said one of his two sons adores sheep and wants to be a shepherd but that now he worries that television may attract him to city life.

The woman, who at first sat very quietly but gradually asserted herself so that by the end she was dominating the conversation, also worried about television but said she adored it and watched it all day. She thought some of it was too sexy but said that doesn't matter; it really doesn't affect things. Sex is a matter of smell and one can tell if the other wants to make love just by smelling it. The shepherd wondered if it was possible to mate a wolf with a dog. Nobody knew anything about the famous ancient Molossian dogs that looked like bears. The Molossians were among the first Epirote people.

After lunch and a nap we went down to the square. The wedding ceremony had been held in church and now the whole party — families and friends — were dancing an endless series of *sirtos*, generally led by the bride, a blonde dressed in white with a white veil held up by a little bridesmaid. The orchestra was full of zip — and drink.

Yanni told me that Greek law forces every adult to vote unless he can produce a valid reason not to. If he has no proof of having voted, he can't do important business like buying or selling a house. He said the trouble with Greek politics is that people only vote for those who promise to help their local regions; they don't care about realities or national interests, only promises.

Dined that night in the stoa, a little group of taverns and shops created by Evanghelos Averof. Ate gobs of souvlakia and drank vast amounts of wine as other guests kept sending us more. Our principal companion — others came and went — was a handsome, burly mechanic with a well-trimmed beard and a powerful build who had been part of our fishing party yesterday. He is an avowed Royalist and says: "The Communists should be put down. They are like a penis. If you caress them, they grow; if you smack them, they wilt."

Christopher and I left Metsovo sadly. Our last stop was the little cheese factory at the end of the village where Yanni came to say farewell and to instruct Apostoli, the young Vlach head of the enterprise, to give me a large chunk of the delicious parmesan, an entire smoked cheese, and some of their local sheep's-milk Gruyère.

We drove off to Kalabáka for lunch and to visit the famed Metéora rocks on which medieval monasteries are perched. In the eleventh century hermits and anchorites took to dwelling in caves like swallow's nests set in these straight igneous pillars that look as if they had been the cores of prehistoric volcanoes, iron-colored towers of rock rising from hills above the plain, absolutely vertical. In the fourteenth century these religious folk were gathered into monasteries atop the rocks as protection against brigands and invaders.

During the long Turkish occupation the monasteries — which were so isolated that food, water, and visitors had to be hauled up on rope windlasses — served as refuges for the persecuted. Now only a handful remain and only about ten monks and twenty nuns still live there.

Kalabáka, which is on the edge of Thessaly — far lower and hotter than Epirus across the Pindus range — belongs itself to the more important but less lovely and interesting Thessalian province. It was so ghastly hot and fly-ridden in Kalabáka that instead of spending the night, I decided to drive on to Delphi where I could be sure of comfort. First we went to Trikkala, in a dusty plain on the site of Homer's Tricca. It was the home of Asclepios and also of a kind of medical center for that god of healing. We drove over the last steep mountain range to Delphi just as the sun had set.

Delphi was wonderful. The majestic vigor of Mount Parnassus, seat of the famous shrine, is especially impressive at sunrise before the mists gather. The whole Gulf of Corinth lies spread out below, while occasional vultures wheel above.

Delphi was regarded by Greeks and others as the center of the classical world and its oracle was the most prestigious. The rock crevasses and precipices had given it an early reputation as sacred to Gaea, goddess of the Earth, and Poseidon. It was then called Pytho, as it is in Homer, and its oracle officiated near the cave of the serpent Python, Gaea's son. Later the cult of Apollo Delphinios (dolphin) was imported from Crete and Pytho became Delphi, Sanctuary of the Pythian Apollo.

In the fifth century B.C. Xerxes sent his Persians to plunder the temple but was foiled by a massive rockfall attributed to divine intervention. After the Peloponnesian and Macedonian wars, Delphi began its decline. The Romans took over and Nero stole over five hundred of its statutes when the oracle condemned his matricide. Julian the Apostate, seeking to reestablish the old faith, consulted the oracle but it was abolished by Theodosius around A.D. 385.

The oracle's methods were peculiarly effective. To consult it, the advice seeker sacrificed an animal, then gathered with others in a room where their priority was decided by the Delphians. Women were not allowed direct access but could hand in questions on leaden tablets. The Pythia, or priestess speaking for the oracle, was always an elderly peasant woman who purified herself by munching laurel leaves and drinking from the sacred Castalian Spring, then seated herself on a tripod above a chasm, uttering incoherent sounds which were shrewdly interpreted in hexameter lines by a poet in attendance. His words were both obscure and equivocal, leading to a reputation for accuracy that could, of course, be misinterpreted by folly.

The shrine had political and social importance. The Pythian Games were held every four years to honor Apollo and his victory over the serpent. The theater featured concerts, comedies, and tragedies. The main Greek city states each had a treasury in their name where gifts were housed. The principal monuments and buildings were linked by a sacred way. Many of the old Greek battles were celebrated by donations — the spoils of Marathon and Plataea, for example.

Yesterday I wandered through all this glory — now terribly ruined, with few exceptions — while Christopher, although he lives in Mount Parnassus (Paris) already, had to remain tethered to the gatekeeper's fencepost. The museum has several fascinating objects, including friezes of Castor and Pollux, the twin sons of Zeus, and their shipmate Orpheus on the ship *Argo*; as well as the Golden Fleece it sought. In the first room are three massive bronze shields which must have required strong men to bear them as well, and also bronze helmets, some appearing battered in by clubs. But the two most magnificent single items are a marble statue of Agias, a champion pankratist (combined wrestling and boxing), which is said to be a copy of a bronze original; and the marvelous bronze charioteer standing at the reins just after winning a race, trotting his horses about on a ceremonial round.

We left, descending the steep slope to Itéa and Galaxidi and driving on along the Gulf of Corinth's northern shore to Naupactos and the ferry to the Peloponnesos. From there we drove through Aigion where with much difficulty we were able to get a lunch of roast lamb from an antidog restaurant, then past ancient Acrocorinth which had been a wealthy and almost impregnable trading post. As is often the case with prosperous centers, it was famous for its licentiousness and vices.

From there to Nemea, where Hercules slew the Nemean lion, and then on across the Argolic plain to Mycenae, capital of King Agamemnon. After a night in a horrible, smelly, hot hotel in Mycenae, which Christopher enjoyed as little as I, having had to be smacked for trying to run away from strange noises, we rose at 6:30 A.M. and went off to the ruins. They are as impressive as ever and meant even more to me after having seen Michael Cacoyannis's remarkable movie, *Iphigénie*. Mycenae, on a fairly low rocky height, was the center of the powerful Helladic civilization. In those days, the fort commanded the Port of Nauplia, although today it is nine miles from the sea. Homer called it "rich in gold" and "broad-streeted," showing how relative everything is.

It was first known as a human habitation around 3,000 B.C. and by 1,500 B.C. had become renowned for its huge *tholos* (beehive) tombs, of which that thought to be Agamemnon's — a high vaulted structure in a hill — is the most famous. About 1350 B.C. the great Lion Gate was built of enormous slabs of rock. The Mycenaean civilization waxed in 1650 B.C. and virtually ceased around 1100 B.C.

It had a cult of the dead who were buried with weapons and much gold, leading to suspicions that their soldiers served as mercenaries for Egypt, whose pharaohs paid commanders in gold. Representations of cheetahs and ostrich eggs have been found in Mycenaean graves. But there are also many Cretan influences — Minoan pottery and representations of bulls — and there is some speculation that Cretan ships ferried these Achaean mercenaries to and from Egypt.

There is increasing reason to suspect that Homer was historically quite right about Mycenaean participation in the siege of Troy, which is now dated at approximately 1240 B.C. If not Agamemnon himself, some thirteenth-century B.C. Mycenaean king played a leading role and Aeolis, where the ships against Troy were assembled, has a Mycenaean cemetery. The Treasury of Atreus, often called Agamemnon's tomb, was built around 1300 B.C.

Then, still in the morning cool before the hot sun embraced the plain, we drove to Argos, famed for its horses and whose citizens were called "Argives" by Homer (like "Danaean" and "Achaean," a synonym for "Greek"). It is named for the mythical Danaos who fled his brother Aegyptos. One of his descendants, Diomedes, led the Argive contingent against Troy and was second only to Achilles as the bravest hero in the besieging contingent.

The next place we stopped was Tiryns, a limestone fortress-town on a knoll. Called "wall-girt Tiryns" by Homer, it is famous for its elaborate palace, and as the legendary birthplace of Hercules. Its system of gateways and fortifications is similar to Mycenae's and it also had underground cisterns secretly fed by springs.

Our final touristic halt was Nauplia, the ancient naval station of Argos, founded by Poseidon's mythical son Nauplios, one of whose descendants, Palamedes, is credited with inventing lighthouses, navigation measures, and the games of dice and knucklebones.

In medieval times Argos had a checkered career. After Constantinople fell to the Normans in 1204, it remained in Byzantine hands for a time. It was taken by Geoffroi de Villehardouin, sold a century later to Venice, became the Ottoman capital in the Morea in the sixteenth century and thereafter was variously occupied by Turks, Venetians, and Russians. Capodistrias briefly made it his capital of free Greece, and King Otho, the first king, disembarked there in 1833.

When we had finally arrived at home in Spetsais I wrote: "We have been back here almost a week now and — apart from the fleas and ticks — Christopher is happy to be re-Hellenized. Yesterday it occurred to me while I was having a beer and sharing a grilled octopus with him in a tiny tavern near the harbor that he must be the only beagle alive who likes eating octopus. That, after all, is a distinction.

"His swimming continues to lag. He goes into the water readily and of his own free will these hot days but is generally out again within two or three minutes. From then on he faithfully follows me along the shore as I strike out on my own or, if he gets bored, goes back and sits on his towel awaiting my return.

"He now has a girlfriend visiting — Sophie Solomos, a spaniel — and is delighted, having been unconsciously or subconsciously a bit mournful because his greatest pal, a large mongrel we all called Oscar, and whom he adored, seems to have died during the winter. Poor Oscar, whose owner we never discovered, appeared to exist on scraps and was always very timid about coming into our garden. But once he got there, I regret to say, he delighted in peeing all over the place, indoors and out — a discouraging habit because it was swiftly emulated by the admiring Christopher."

VII   One July night I took Christopher for dinner at the home of my young friends Caroline and Adonis Kyrou. Caroline is a charming French girl and Adonis is publisher of the right-wing Athens newspaper *Estia*. He is also an enthusiastic sea diver, both for fish and underwater archaeology. He showed me a handful of two-hundred-year-old Turkish pipes that the two of them had just found off the Peloponnesian coast.

It was a small party and Christopher had his own special small table — although I wouldn't allow him any food while the rest of us gorged on an excellent meal, starting with a huge lobster Adonis had arranged with a fisherman friend to catch and save for him. Present were Nikos Gialouris, inspector general of the Greek Archaeological Service, and Professor Wolf Rudolph, a West German — born in Poznań but brought up in Kiel — who is also an archaeologist. He is thirty-seven years old, now a member of the faculty of Indiana University at Bloomington and in charge of a Proto-Helladic dig they are doing near Porto-Cheli, on the mainland almost opposite Spetsais.

It was an exceptionally pleasant evening. Gialouris is enthusiastic about my idea of a Whole Earth Museum containing in one building the best samples of eternal Greece. He promised to urge it upon Evanghelos Averof after I see him next week in Athens. He is ready to promote a system whereby Greek museums contribute their prize pieces to such a museum in exchange for copies or for other works.

I was struck by the way they all regard the Troy of King Priam, destroyed in the twelfth-century B.C. Trojan War, as relatively modern. Some of the ruins excavated there go back to about 3500 B.C. They talked of the effect of the horse on history. It came to these parts from Asia between 3000 and 2000 B.C. and was first used only to draw vehicles, like chariots, not for riding.

Christopher was more interested in the food he didn't get than in the conversation he did. He got his revenge by running away at midnight when I took off his chain on the way home, returning a half hour later (I'd left the door open) to see if I was okay, then taking off again until 2:30 A.M. when he woke me up by jumping up on the bed.

I took the boat to Athens to see Evanghelos Averof, defense minister. Christopher came along for the boat ride but even on a hot summer day he doesn't stick his head up to benefit from the cool breeze or to examine the lovely seascape. An odd dog.

I spent an hour and a half with Averof. The purpose of the visit was to get him moving on my Whole Earth Museum which has never yet caught hold here in Greece, for which it is conceived. He was immensely enthusiastic at the start but then began to waver a bit and tell me about all the problems that would inevitably arise. I said any great project always had many problems and that if he kept his eye on the final goal, it would be the greatest achievement in Greece for centuries.

Shortly after our return to Spetsais, Stavros Niarchos invited me to lunch. I took my daughter, Marinette, who was delighted, but not Christopher, who was not appeased by the explanation that Stavros's island, Spetsopoula, is filled with large and hostile hunting dogs. Nicko and Mary Henderson, who were holidaying here, joined us in the Niarchos motor launch.

We whizzed over in great style across a slightly choppy sea. A shooting brake was waiting and drove us to the main house where Stavros has built a lovely kidney-shaped swimming pool. He was sitting there in trunks, working in the sun, a telephone on an automatic rewinding spool of wire beside him. He explained that he uses this as an office when he can.

He then showed us through the house, which the others had never seen. The large living room is fantastic. At one end a special section of wooden walls from an 1838 Swiss barn (he has a house in St. Moritz) has been most tastefully inserted. There is stationed Picasso's famous *Harlequin* of the pink-and-blue period. He also owns a lovely Rouault, two Van Goghs, two Modiglianis, a Toulouse-Lautrec, a Gauguin, a Renoir, a Manet (small study for *Olympia*) and two small Delacroixs. And, of course, he has incredible additional treasures, including two El Grecos, in Paris, St. Moritz, and elsewhere.

The house is a curious mixture. It is filled with hunting trophies from Africa, heads, tusks, mounted beasts. Also some fine icons, especially an incredible small fifteenth-century Byzantine one composed of tiny pieces of mosaic, mostly gold. His study is of unvarnished pine which smells delightfully of resin. Here he has two indoor exercise bicycles, one of which has computer buttons which you push according to your age, weight, etc. and then, after you've ridden it ten minutes, it tells you what sort of condition you are in on that particular day. Stavros looks lean and hard, fitter than I've seen him in years, although he's now sixty-nine. He has virtually given up drinking, except a little wine. He has also given up shooting, save three or four times a year, because of ear trouble. Now at most he keeps about nine thousand partridges and a few mouflon. He says even this small amount requires one seven-hundred-ton tanker of water every two days, for the game and gamekeepers.

In his bedroom, beside the large double bed rested a pile of books and magazines, including art catalogues for auctions and also some erotica. I noticed on the first shelf above his bed a book on his worst enemy and late brother-in-law, Onassis.

When we arrived at the swimming beach, Stavros's eldest son, Philip, showed him the day's news (he has a private news ticker), including confirmation that his niece and former stepdaughter, Christina Onassis, is marrying Kauzov, a Russian, almost forty. Stavros sneers that "the most" Kauzov can get his hands on is about $200 million in cash and other assets. The fifteen large Onassis tankers are all chartered for a decade to come. I asked what Onassis was worth. He said: "At his death, about $500 million; but that value has fallen since." It seems to my modest taste that $200 million of this is a pleasant windfall for the KGB, for whom, says Stavros, the happy groom works. He has only one eye; but that's not what he makes love with.

First we swam and then had preprandial drinks. All the time we were at lunch, the phone by Stavros's side kept ringing, with a canarylike chirp, and he had numerous brief business conversations in Greek. He showed me a folder listing the present positions of his ships. He receives about one hundred and twenty reports daily from his vessels at sea.

The next day was splendid: hot and cloudless, with a cool sea;

then a cool evening with a breeze. Took Christopher for a morning walk to get the logyness out of him. He had celebrated the night by raiding a broken icebox, cleverly forcing his way in and consuming four huge raw hamburgers. Today he is like a small hippopotamus.

We walked around the little shipyard where carpenters still build large caiques as they have been doing since Homer's time. The boat frames are on stilts; the ribs are all shaped; planks are hammered to them. They are painted orange against the elements.

Just before reaching the shipyard and the repair yard, where yachts are fixed up, and then the row of moored boats in the Old Port (Palio Limani), we admired the long lines of yellow, fine mesh nets set out to dry by the local fishermen. Christopher wanted to stop and eat grilled octopus at a tavern. Not after the hamburger raid — and dozens of his favorite fried whitebait (merides) at a drinks party we gave yesterday.

Went swimming at the Woodses' jetty where Christopher attacked a large black hound named Tarzan and got the equivalent of a black eye (bitten under the right eye) for his pains. As usual, Christopher was the aggressor. For some reason he only attacks dogs larger than he is.

In the evening Marinette took a group of us to the theater at Epidaurus, the fourth-century B.C. theater which holds fourteen thousand people. We went on a special travel agency tourist deal — boat across to Costa, then air-conditioned bus to Epidaurus, theater, and return.

It is a lovely theater and well sheltered by large pines and flowers. The sky was filled with scudding clouds and it got quite cold. The play was Sophocles' *Oedipus Rex* as put on by the Greek Art Theater. It was a splendid sight and the audience sat fascinated despite the hard stone, backless, seats.

Winston and Minnie Churchill came for drinks. Winston said Vladimir Bukovsky, the Soviet dissident, told him he was first picked up by the KGB for possessing a copy of Djilas's book *The New Class.* Bukovsky also told him that he had been astonished to find handcuffs in Soviet prisons stamped "made in USA."

In August, on a brief motor trip toward Paris, I spent a couple of hours with Costa Caramanlis, the prime minister. I took Christopher along and he was royally treated by the prime ministerial staff.

We talked about Turkey and the U.S. move lifting the Turkish arms embargo. He said: "Although I am against that, I appreciate the fact that Congress attached certain conditions which might facilitate solution of the Cyprus problem and preserve the peace in the Aegean area. If these congressional conditions are respected by the administration, we consider the congressional move useful."

Caramanlis said Greece has social calm and in four years no one has been killed in strikes, riots, or social strife. There is no terrorism nor anarchy as in other countries. He added: "I suppose I'm the only prime minister in Europe who walks home, goes swimming with others on the beach, dines in taverns with friends."

Of the Carter administration he said: "I don't like to criticize but its weak point today is that it doesn't have a stable, fixed policy. Its policy isn't clear on any big issue. And today everyone insults America abroad: the opposition parties, the press. There is no U.S. reaction to these attacks, no statements contradicting them. Maybe the U.S. has a superiority complex. But lies should be denounced."

He said: "There is an incoherence in the West right now. If this is not corrected, it will justify Marx's view that capitalism will destroy itself. After all, the eastern European countries, although they have problems, don't have unrest, strikes, terrorism, inflation. They control their problems; the West doesn't."

We drove from Athens early in the morning for Salonika where Caramanlis had arranged for me to be received by Nikolaos Martis, minister for northern Greece (Macedonia and Thrace), who would take us on to the excavations of Philip of Macedon and Alexander the Great.

Off we went under the range of Mount Olympus and Ossa, down the lovely Peniós River through the beautiful, narrow Vale of Tempe. We passed the great castle of Platamona, erected by the sea by Crusaders in the thirteenth century to command the Thermaic Gulf, which had been taken by the Greeks from Lombard troops who fell from the walls "like birds from their nest."

On into Macedonia, which has only been under the sovereignty of modern Greece since 1912, and into Salonika along the same route as the Via Egnatia, which went from Valona and Durazzo to Byzantium.

During the subsequent hours we were in several former Macedonian capitals including Pella, where Alexander the Great was born; Vergina, formerly called Aegae, where his father, Philip II, is buried; Edessa, from where the whole region was subdued by Perdiccas, in the seventh century B.C.; and, of course, Salonika, named for Thessalonikeia, half-sister of Alexander and wife of the founder, Cassander. Later the second city of the Byzantine empire and the scene of Saint Paul's preachments, it became a center for the thousands of Jews expelled by Spain in 1492 who, in the sixteenth century, formed the majority of the population, speaking Ladino — Castillian written in Hebrew letters. The young Turk movement which revolted against the sultan in 1908 was formed there.

First drove to the residence of Martis, high on a bluff over the gulf; had orange juice and then on we went, he riding in my Volkswagen while his large chauffeur-driven Mercedes followed. Christopher made the best of the opportunity (the back being jammed with luggage) and climbed all over the minister so he emerged looking like an abominable snowman, with white beagle hair front, back, and sides all over.

At the Salonika museum — small but spacious and in exquisite taste — a woman guide met us and took us through the rooms containing discoveries from the excavations at Vergina by Professor Manolis Andronikos. She said Macedonia and especially the western part, near the Pindus, was the first region known to Greek tribes descending from central Europe during the second millennium B.C. They came down from Pieria toward the valley and founded their first capital, Aegae, which was later replaced by Pella.

The displays are fantastic: two large square ossuary boxes of almost pure gold, engraved and studded, that contained bones from burned royal bodies and diadems of golden oak leaves and acorns; early crowns, weapons (helmets, spearheads, swords with ivory and gold hilts, golden arrow quivers, all carved and hammered), coins, statuettes, jewelry, and more. It was a very wealthy civilization and even the poorest people were well off because of the richness of the land.

In Vergina, although it was getting dark, Professor Andronikos and a team were waiting for us. We followed Martis's car and it was somewhat embarrassing. I had put Christopher on a suitcase behind and he lay there farting silently but smellily. I couldn't reprove him because Martis might think I thought that he was actually the culprit, or that it was really me, pretending by fixing the blame elsewhere. It reminded me of the time I saw Tito in 1946 and Tiger, his police dog, lay doing the same thing until both Tito and I, who were having a frigid conversation (it was a moment of crisis with the United States) burst out laughing and he pushed a button, summoned *slivovica*, and the ice was broken.

At Vergina, Andronikos, a charming, agile, bearded old man, took us to a tomb that had just been opened the previous day (I was the first outside visitor). It had been covered by more than forty feet of earth. Part of two frescoes had been found. The first was beginning to fade because vegetable matter had decomposed. Professor Andronikos said there were several great painters at the time — fourth century B.C. — who wandered among different courts, taking jobs for which they were richly paid. Hardly any paintings have been found intact. Many tombs had been robbed. This tomb was for a member of Philip's family. We then went into Philip's larger tomb, also with fine paintings. Aegae was a great cemetery for the royal Macedonian family and contains the only frescoes found in Greece. One clearly shows hunting dogs, deer, spearmen. The ancient odors had Christopher's nostrils twitching.

Andronikos took us into a room where his experts are putting together tiny fragments into their original form; especially a large round shield of wood, leather and cloth, with gold and ivory decorations, used only for ceremonials. He said it is evident that the Macedonians were a true Greek people; their common soldiers as well as dozens of generals had Greek names. The word "Macedonia" means "big people," however, they were small compared to us, as can be seen from their leg greaves.

We then drove in the dark through Véroia, where Pompey spent the winter of 49 to 48 B.C. and which has numerous wattle-and-timber churches, camouflaged against the occupying Turks; past Náousa (once Nea Augusta), famous for its peaches and red wine, to Pella. Pella is renowned for its large, beautiful mosaic floors (fourth century B.C.) of which I saw, by lamplight, a lion hunt, Dionysus on a leopard's back, griffin attacking a deer, and the rape of Helen. In the small museum there is a handsome marble statue of a hound, carved for a tomb, and hounds appear in hunting scenes. Christopher was most interested in these ancestral relics.

Finally we left Martis and persevered on to Edessa, guided by a police car with a revolving blue light. Edessa was made into the capital by Perdiccas, first Macedonian king, and remained so until Pella took over in the fourth century B.C. Philip II was assassinated in Edessa in 336 B.C. It is beautiful, in low mountains with streams and waterfalls, cliffs covered with luxuriant vegetation, nuts, wines, pomegranates, figs. There is a cave with stalactites, and crayfish in the water, and an old bridge that bore the Via Egnatia.

Next day, still guided by a series of Greek police cars, we drove through a landscape of round green mountains and lakes, with orchards spread along the intervening valleys, emerging on golden plateaus of corn and harvested-wheat stubble.

Finally entered Florina, an ugly town at the Greek (southern) end of the broad Monastir Gap leading to Jugoslavia and Bitola, on the eastern slope of a mountain range. The last two times I'd been in Florina were in April 1941 and September 1946. In 1941 I was in an open Mercedes escaping from Jugoslavia and the Nazis. Entering Florina I passed the last Jugoslav unit to escape as Luftwaffe planes cruised overhead. The road was part cobbled and part dirt. There were no frontier or customs guards on either side. The main German army was on my heels.

In 1946 I was in a jeep that I had driven from Rome. I saw Tito in Belgrade and then took off with a revolver hung behind the dashboard to protect the vehicle. There was civil war in Greece and the Četniks had not yet been wiped out in Jugoslavia. At the border the Jugoslav commander warned me not to go because the stretch of dirt road between Greece and Jugoslavia had never been swept of mines nor crossed by a vehicle since the Germans had evacuated Greece. When I insisted, he ordered some of his soldiers to pack the jeep's floor with hastily stuffed sandbags as some protection against blast. I had no trouble, however, once I persuaded nervous Greek patrols I was American and not an invading Jugoslav (the two neighbors were near war then as Tito backed the Communist rebels in Greece).

Now I was once again in a German-made car, this time a Volkswagen Passat. It was not the first time I had had a dog with me. I used to travel with Felix, my wirehaired fox terrier, when I would rush down for occasions like Christmas bearing gifts for

Marina, whom I was courting. Felix and Marina are long gone. It is a lonelier journey, even with Christopher's best efforts at cheer.

VIII Although a Marxist state, Jugoslavia is immensely relaxed compared with the Soviet bloc, and formalities at the frontier are minimal. We rumbled over a cobbled road to Bitola (the Macedonian spelling by which the former Bitolj — Serbian spelling — is now known). In Bitola it was impossible to get lunch since no restaurant would admit Christopher. I was astounded. Christopher's law: the south of a country is anticanine. The revolution has been hard on dogs. In the old pre-Tito days, I often took Felix to the movies in Jugoslavia, buying him a child's ticket.

Finally found lunch for both of us in a modest country tavern by the roadside. Ordered *raznici* (souvlakia) for Christopher and *čevabčiči* (meatballs) for me, grateful that we seemed less doomed to die of starvation. I then took him for a walk in a lovely field but when I released him from the leash he started to trot off for the distant car; I caught him just in time.

Drove on toward Ohrid over ranges of wooded mountains. Ohrid is still a tranquil, dreamy place which the government has preserved well although it has swollen in size. Many of the old stone-and-wood, wood, or plaster-and-wood overhanging houses have been repaired or rebuilt and the famous churches are nicely cared for although not, apparently, used for religious purposes anymore. There are willows in the town and an absolutely enormous split and hollow tree — low but of about twenty feet circumference at the base — in an old square.

After finding a room at last in the modern, pretentious Hotel Metropol, with terrible service but a pleasant view of the wide Lake Ohrid, we drove off sightseeing. First the basilica of Saint

Sofia — eleventh-century Romanesque with some fine murals, mostly in fragments — softly echoing to recorded ecclesiastical music. Then to thirteenth-century Saint Clément, containing relics of this saint who, with Saint Naum, was one of the two successors of Saint Cyril and Saint Methodius, who brought Greek Christianity to the Slavs. It is on a hilltop below the crest marked by the ruined fortress of the Bulgarian tsar Samuel, who built it in the tenth century where a Byzantine citadel had stood.

Then we drove twenty miles south, almost into Albania, where we visited the monastery of Saint Naum. I had stayed there in January, 1939 as guest of the abbot, after leaving Albanian Pogradec in a snowstorm by rowboat. He and I used to sit up drinking *slivovica* and smoking American cigarettes the U.S. minister in Tirana had given me. Once I set fire to his booze-soaked beard, lighting up for him, and he patted out the conflagration, not even noticing.

Above the entry door to the building, on a height above the lake, is a fresco of the saint standing upright in a cart with two solid wheels, drawn by two oxen, much like carts I saw on the road bringing in hay. The door to the abbey is of five to six-inch-thick wood, studded with iron. The monastic rooms where I stayed have been converted into a hotel. In the courtyard, bordered by fig trees, is a lovely fourteenth-century church containing the saint's tomb.

The chapel is covered with curling red tiles, overlapping each other in whorls, and contains fine murals. From the wall above the huge lake — famous for its pink-fleshed trout, or char — one can see the cliffed Jugoslav shore to the northeast and the Albanian mountains to the west. The sun was just setting as we left, strolling past a dammed-up pond where a few peacocks strutted and pigeons cooed.

We left Ohrid early the next day, driving through the old quarter. I was reminded of the first dilapidated wooden hotel I'd stayed in forty years ago during a piercing winter. When I arrived I was installed in my room and soon a young Turkish girl came up with a load of firewood for the potbellied stove which was the only source of heat. When she had the flames roaring she slammed the stove door and calmly spread herself on the bed, legs apart, to confer with grace and enthusiasm an even older source of warmth, which I was glad to enjoy after my arduous trip out of Albania and a few days of ascetic hospitality at the monastery of Saint Naum, cut off by a blizzard.

Drove slowly by the great lake past women in traditional Macedonian costume and young men jogging in sweat suits. Christopher promptly assumed his normal car position, hiding in a semifoetal pose in his lair under the dashboard, as we whizzed out of Ohrid toward Skopje. Went past the sideroad to Debar; the old road passed through that largely Albanian village forty years ago. I remember, during that bitter winter with snow all over, going by rickety bus to Skopje and it took all day to get to Debar, now little more than an hour away. We had to stop time and again and all the passengers set to with the driver, shoveling snow out of our way; that is, all but a mournful soldier traveling with his girlfriend. He had a terrible toothache; his jaw was bound up in a scarf; and he simply sat there holding his misery and murmuring, "Oh my mother, my little mother," while his girlfriend joined the shovelers. We had to spend the night in a modest inn at Debar. Next day we bumped on slowly to Skopje.

Today the whole journey took just over two hours on a fine highway through a rich valley, tree-clad mountains, narrow green gorges. Here and there in some towns and villages, like Kičevo, I noted many Albanians with their white felt fezzes or skullcaps.

Road signs pointing to Veles recalled to me passing through that city in April, 1941 while Jugoslavia was being attacked and occupied by the Axis armies. One bridge across the Vardar was down but a railway bridge was still up although in flames. I hauled burning timbers and edged them into the river below, then scuttled across in my little Mercedes convertible, to enter a Veles with no inhabitants, many wrecked houses, and bomb craters in the main street. The Germans took the town shortly afterward.

Finally got into Skopje which is now a big, booming (although ugly) city, having survived destruction in World War II and a recent bad earthquake with remarkable vigor. Again, I remember talking to the commanding general at headquarters in 1941. He was a small Serb with an old-fashioned high uniform collar which he had opened because of a boil on the back of his neck. Having had no food since war began, he was munching a dry crust of bread. Yet, despite chaos everywhere — glass, wreckage, telephone wires, corpses of humans and horses in the streets — he exuded calm confidence. Four hours later he and the city were in German hands.

Alas, now I am too old for Turkish girls and wars. It is all I can do to remember them.

Continued along a magnificent mountain road to Prizren, a route that ended, after climbing high valleys, in a narrow, cliff-girt gorge cut through the rock by a rushing trout stream. The town, ancient and distinguished, is on the edge of a plain but jammed tight up against the steep hills leading to the high mountains. It was a great city under the Nemanjić kings of Serbia in the fourteenth century and even for a while the capital. The Turks conquered it in 1455.

At the entrance from the gorge, on the left, is a crenellated tower on a high peak and below it the ruins of a massive fortress designed by the emperor Dušan in the fourteenth century to protect the Monastery of the Holy Archangels, set within the massive walls. The town contains another medieval fortification and a fine church of Our Lady of Ljeviška built in 1307, with excellent murals. It also boasts a mosque built by Suleiman the Magnificent's great Renaissance architect Sinan.

Across a dismal, hot flat plain lies Peć, a colorful town with many minarets and Albanian shopkeepers. Outside is the fourteenth-century Byzantine monastery of Dečani with some of the finest frescoes produced in the great period of Serbian art. These include portraits of the famous rulers Stefan Dečanski and Dušan Silni.

From Peć we took off across high mountains to Montenegro. The road, quite unsurfaced and covered with sharp rocks, is so ghastly that I blew the right rear tire at some point and rode along on the wheel, fragments of the tire spinning off. I felt no difference. It was all rock and roll, rattle and bang before and after the event. I only discovered it at the top of the pass and, fortunately, Volkswagens have a spare wheel inside the spare tire, for the original wheel was no longer round.

The road through the Morača gorge is absolutely beautiful and utterly wild. One passes very few cars and a trip that might take forty minutes on a good highway takes more than three times that long. Here and there I stopped to water Christopher in the trout stream whose course we followed. There were endless forests, birds, wild flowers; and no people once we had left the old patriarchate of Peć, outside the town where the thirteen-century Saint Sava detached Serbian Orthodoxy from the Greek church.

At last, after what seemed an endless contrast between the horrors of the road and the beauties of the landscape, we emerged at the disgorgement of the Lim River, found a relatively passable path that led onto a good highway and, following the Morača River, drove past the monastery of that name founded in 1251 by Prince Stefan. From there it was no trouble to speed on to Titograd after an arduous ten hours of driving without even stopping for lunch. Christopher was as tired and dusty as I.

Titograd itself, previously known as Podgorica, is the large, uninteresting capital of the Socialist Republic of Montenegro, as Skopje is of the Macedonian Republic. Its outstanding feature is the entry from the east through the breathtaking Morača canyon — narrow and with high, vertical walls.

I got Christopher into a reluctant hotel. The porter said he couldn't eat there and that no restaurant in town would serve him. It so happened the first I tried did. He dined well on steak and meatballs. Then we took a long cool walk through the park, embraced by evening breezes.

We came out of the park on a street banned to automobiles which was clearly Titograd's version of the Mediterranean *corso* where young girls and lads stroll and flirt in the evenings. We strolled and the girls flirted with Christopher who was feeling a bit tired; tail down and nervous. The boys showed off by whistling shrilly at him or asking in pigeon German, "How old is the hound?" The girls were pathetic: dressed up in homemade finery at least a generation out of date, with smeared lipstick and badly dyed hair. But, despite everything, the Montenegrins are a handsome, sturdy, healthy-looking people.

Onward next day from Titograd to Cetinje after first spending a tedious hour in hot parks watering Christopher. It is a splendid drive far above the Morava valley with its bright blue water and banks of green lilies and weeds. Above are endless grey limestone cliffs and volcanic-looking, cone-shaped peaks covered in green, looking more like South America than the Balkans. For sheer masses of rock and awe-inspiring declivities Montenegro is of the same ilk as the Andean and Himalayan states.

Cetinje, the old capital, is set high on a small, semiplateau, nobbled among the mountains. It is more a village than a town, with rows of old-fashioned low houses (rebuilt after the war) and the former palace of King Nicholas, the popular last ruler of independent Montenegro. The tiny land first proclaimed its independence after the Serbian defeat by Turkey at Kosovo in 1389. For one century it was governed by lay princes, then by the *vladikas* or prince bishops of whom the most famous, Peter II, died in 1851 after writing the classic Serbian poem, "Mountain Wreath."

The last prince, Nicholas, became king in 1910 but emigrated to France when his country was invaded by Austro-Hungarian troops in World War I. In 1918 an assembly at Podgorica proclaimed Montenegro's incorporation into the new South Slav union (Jugoslavia today).

There is little to see in Cetinje except its monastery (founded in 1484, but often rebuilt), the museum in old Nicholas's palace, and Njegoš's (Peter II) "Billiard Palace," named for the first billiard table said to have been imported into the Balkans.

Then down to Budva, on the Adriatic coast, renowned as a base for Illyrian pirates who taunted the Romans, later captured for Justinian by the famous general Belisarius. It was successively under Serbia, Montenegro and Venice, giving some idea of the course of "nationalism" and "frontiers" in this area. Now it is a sleepy fishing village and summer resort.

We wound up for the evening in Saint Stefan, once a little fort north of Ulcinj, the famous Turkish slave market where Sinan built another of his exquisite mosques. I remember in 1938 seeing a black, or mulatto, captain in the Jugoslav army idling with other Serbian officers on the Belgrade Corso. He spoke only Serbian and was a pure Jugoslav — from Ulcinj. His original Balkan ancestor was a slave cabin boy who swam ashore from the wrecked ship of a famous raider, Haralampa. The local Ulcinj people liked him so much they arranged to buy him a negress bride; black families descended from this couple have thrived in the area ever since.

We took a long walk at sundown. The steep hillsides are covered with oak and olives. The mainland is filled with new villas and two deluxe hotels. The tiny islet of St. Stefan is jammed with closely built stone houses and narrow stone alleys, all looking as if made by a jeweler, not an architect. The entire island is one hotel, Sveti Stefan, in the best possible taste, with a pair of beaches on the mainland on each side of the connecting mole.

Started off August 23 along the lovely winding coast road, then climbed upward to see the austere vertical bulk of Lovćen, the famous Montenegrin mountain, with Kotor nestled below on the edge of its vast bay like a sheet of dark green glass. When I think that after Tito's death this area might fall into Soviet hands, I'm frightened. Saseno, the naval base on an island in Valona Bay in Albania, which everyone talked about after Mussolini fortified it, is peanuts compared to what this might be. Saseno could even be shelled by long-range guns from Italy today; but Kotor is entirely impregnable to prenuclear-missile weapons and easier to supply than the U.S. base in Suda Bay, Crete.

Boka Kotorska, the bay, is beautiful and dotted with tiny off-shore islets with sweet Renaissance churches on them, reflected in the tranquil water. After Kotor, Montenegro ends and Croatia begins. Next comes Herceg Novi, an Adriatic village named for a duke, or *herceg*, and successively governed by the seigneurs of Hercegovina, the Turks, the Genoese, and the Ottomans, who seized it under their famous admiral, Barbarossa.

Then on to Dubrovnik, the "pearl of the Adriatic," a beautifully built walled town jutting into the sea on a small peninsula below the bleak limestone cliff formation known as "karst" and clumps of pines, cypress, olives, laurels, palms, and carobs.

Dubrovnik was founded when the nearby town known today as Cavtat, originally called Epidaurus and named for the Greek city, was seized by the Slavs in the seventh century and refugees built a haven on what was then a rocky offshore islet. Under its first name, Ragusa, it fought off Arab fleets, fell to the Normans of the Kingdom of Naples, negotiated with the Grand Župan of Serbia, was dominated by Venice, then by the king of Hungary, maintained tribute-paying independence under the Turks, fell to Napoleon's French (when all the nobles of Dubrovnik foreswore having more children) and finally became Austrian. Its Rectors' Palace by Michelozzo probably inspired the fifteenth-century restoration of Florence's Palazzo Vecchio.

I was astounded to see Dubrovnik yesterday. The walls are far thicker and more solid than I had remembered. The city has now been built up in all directions and threatens to disappear from sight. And the traffic jams and parking blight equal Coney Island. After leaving, I took Christopher for lunch in a small village on the coast, rather shabby and third-rate. The little restaurant where we ate outdoors only agreed to serve anything to him because one of the owner's girls liked Christopher. But he was not allowed to eat off a plate and had water in an ashtray. From this derives another Christopher's Law: the less personal hygiene people have the more worried they are about touching dogs.

We continued to Split which I first visited before World War II arriving by a boat from Rijeka, loaded with turkeys, and tottering down a sixteen-inch-wide rail-less gangplank, bearing my luggage, to be met by my friend Berislav Andjelinović. Noticing several corpses lying about on an otherwise calm scene I asked: "What's going on? What are all the bodies?"

Said Berislav: "Oh, it's election day. We always kill more people in a Jugoslav election than the Greeks do during a revolution." Non sequitur! Berislav, a lawyer, poet, diplomat (and, during the war, successively a Četnik and a partisan), was met by Ivan Frangeš from the Jugoslav Legation in Washington, when he arrived at New York to take a post at the capital. Ivan took him to the Empire State Building to see the view. Berislav walked solemnly round and round, saying nothing, until finally, after several minutes, he announced in a loud voice: "My, what a wonderful city to destroy."

Split is another fantastic place. A pre-Christian Greek colony, it was selected in the third century A.D. by Diocletian as the site of his great palace, an enormous edifice. The city was later built right into its walls. Now, unfortunately, it has grown and grown and the palace has diminished accordingly, unless one arrives by boat and can see it, as I first did, by approaching shore in a vessel and staring right at it. Split contains several statues by Ivan Meštrović, including the huge *Bishop Gregory of Nin*.

Both tired, we whizzed on once more toward Zadar where we

hoped to spend the night. Traffic was murderous but at last we reached Zadar, known as Zara prior to 1945 when Jugoslavia was awarded it after Italy's defeat. It had been an Italian enclave on the East Adriatic coast. It has importance as a port and manufacturing center and also as the original fabricating center of Maraschino (Maraska) and its cherries. The Maraska company makes various liqueurs now; the original Zara Italian distillers fled to Italy with their formula.

Zadar was first known as the Roman Iadera, taken from the Illyrian tribe of Liburnians. In the fifth century it fell to marauding Goths and then became part of the Byzantine empire. Croats moved in in the eighth century and in the ninth century, Zadar paid tribute to Charlemagne and his Franks, after Bishop Donat made obeisance as a vassal. The Fourth Crusade passed through Zadar, and Venice ruled it (with a Hungarian interlude) until Napoleon's troops took it.

We spent the night there, first trying one hotel which was so disagreeable and anti-Christopher that we walked out. Our discovery that the further south in a country one goes the worse people are to dogs isn't always true, as Zadar is fairly far north. I guess it's more a question of education and wealth. Good hotels and restaurants treat him well; bad hotels and restaurants would kick him if they could. At the hotel we walked out of, when I asked at the restaurant if they could serve me outside, the nasty headwaiter said: "*Kein hund,*" and turned his back insolently. Maybe the Fascists were here too long; at least that's Christopher's theory. However, once we were established in another and better hotel he played his usual "Pied Piper of Dogdom" game and all the children in the place swarmed around him in glee.

We looked about Zadar in the morning before moving northward. There are several things to see, including the thirteenth-century Church of Saint Francis with a fine gothic cloister where Christopher admired the coolness and the smell of death seeping out of the gruesome skull-and-bones tombstones. Then walked around the eleventh-to-twelfth-century Cathedral of Saint Anastasia with roped, Romanesque stone arches. Finally visited the ninth-century church of Saint Donat with towering walls and windows about forty feet above the ground, looking like a fortress.

We toured the harbor where some sailors still wear the red-topped, black-rimmed Dalmatian pillbox cap, and women are in national costume. Zadar is not geographically up to the high standard of the Dalmatian coast; it is a low, mosquitoey peninsula with brackish, polluted, still water. But the old town is beautifully made by Italian architects, with every stone carefully joined, even the polished paving blocks.

We drove on by romantic little Rab, a Roman naval base that changed hands among rival rulers many times, as was common in this region. Across the water, below the grey karst, the islands looked like great, tan, basking walruses. Traversed Senj, famous to me for its romantic hero, Ivo, of the old guslar (blind bard) lays, who was killed at Kosovo fighting the Turks. For a long time the so-called *uskoks*, or escapees, who had fled the Turks from fortresses near Split, practiced a continual pirate war against Venetian and Turkish ships and forts.

We wound up going through Rijeka. When I first knew it, this comprised Fiume, under Italy, and a small suburb under Jugoslavia called Rijeka. Now it is all one Jugoslav port. I passed through twice in 1938, once when the Stojadinović dictatorship threw me out of Jugoslavia for daring to interview Vlatko Maček, the Croat peasant leader; and again on my way back after Belgrade backed down.

Finally we lunched at a village in the hills above Rijeka, Christopher ordering and consuming a plate of mixed grill, which delighted the local children. Drove on through Ljubljana and a cloudburst thunderstorm, worried about what I'd do if a tire failed, as I'd lost my spare and its wheel — utterly demolished by the Peč-Kolašin road. (I had also lost my typewriter, dropped by a clumsy oaf at Zadar.) Finally crossed the border near Jesenice.

I first came through Jesenice in 1938 after a wait of many hours on a siding at Mallnitz, when Austria was part of Hitler's Germany. Finally the Munich sellout came and the troop trains that had been whizzing past, monopolizing the tracks, ceased long enough for us to proceed to Jugoslavia. In the town of Jesenice, soldiers were still being called up because the Jugoslavs were slow to recognize the cessation of a war threat. People were singing, weeping, and above all, drinking, as each soldier was embraced and kissed by everyone before being poured aboard.

On emerging from Jugoslavia with Christopher, I couldn't help but experience relief, much as I love it. The bureaucracy is stupidly inefficient. Everything is for the bureaucrats, nothing for the customer. You have to go to a bank to change money; the hotel can't be bothered, although it's for their bill. I couldn't call Zadar from Sveti Stefan because the operator was out when the government bureaucrat in charge of reservations was in; and vice versa. There are so few gas stations it takes a half hour queuing to fill up.

In Austria, we spent a very comfortable night at the Moser Hotel in Klagenfurt where both of us were made heartily welcome. Christopher was served on plates and in bowls and the dining room personnel vied for the privilege.

I remember when Tito told me in 1945, while the war was still on, that Jugoslavia was laying claim to Klagenfurt and the territory around it. There are indeed Slovenes as well as Teutons in the hinterland, but that kind of mixture was one of the best features of the old Austro-Hungarian Empire in which Tito grew up, served as a test driver for Daimler-Benz, and fought as a soldier during the battle against Belgrade before being shifted to the Russian front where he was taken prisoner. Well, there are similar mixtures on all European borders. Ethnicity can't be cut with a knife.

And although Slovenia is the most "European" of all the Jugo-slav republics, Klagenfurt, a small Austrian town and capital of Carinthia, is more "European" than any Slovenian city. By far. Ask Christopher. An honored guest in all restaurants he entered, he was fondled, dandled, and given water without asking. "The hell with the vital primitive Balkans," he says, "where men are heroes and dogs are curs. Give me the soft, spoiled, decadent West." The Austrians are clean and not obsessed by germs like the Jugoslavs who perhaps carry theirs with them.

As for me, I told the lady concierge on arriving after sundown that I would leave my broken typewriter with her to send off to be repaired extra fast in the morning. And I got the address of a Volkswagen dealer to get a new wheel and tire. Next morning, believe it or not, although the dealer was three kilometers out of town, I had the wheel and tire within a half hour. And the typewriter was back in perfect condition within three hours. That beats Paris by far.

Despite tight traffic, thanks to the autoroutes along much of the way, we got to Salzburg within two and a half hours. A cheesy hotel, but who cares. To get anything there in August is a tri-umph. Late lunch in an out-of-doors *Bier Keller*. For me, two frankfurters; for Christopher, a grilled steak. I took Christopher on a stroll through this famous center of the arts and, above all, music. We wandered by the concert hall and, next door, the Mozarteum where the great composer lived. Crowds, for the most part respectfully dressed in evening clothes, were entering. We then went by the famous marionette theater and the re-nowned Festspielhaus. We continued along the right bank of the Salzach River where it flows below the height crowned by a large castle. It is a truly baroque city — like Prague. A baroque mu-seum, near a baroque park filled with baroque statues.

Next day, we drove on to Munich and, skirting it, on to Lake Constance, or Bodensee. As we passed signs pointing to Dachau, outside Munich, I thought that no dogs ever did to each other what the Nazi version of mankind did to the human race. I remembered early 1938 when I was in Vienna after Hitler took it, and John Wiley, the brave U.S. consul-general (ex-minister to independent Austria, later an ambassador) told me of information he had gathered about train loads, mostly Jews, shipped north in locked freight cars and how, when the cars got back to Vienna, they were splattered with blood and sometimes contained gobs of flesh.

We then passed close to Landsberg, the grim fortress where Hitler was imprisoned after the futile Munich beer-hall putsch and where he wrote *Mein Kampf.* On to Lindau, for more than five centuries a free imperial city under the Holy Roman Emperor. Some of my ancestors came from this region and it is interesting to me that there are many Sulzbergers dwelling on both the German and Swiss sides of the lake area and that they are Catholic, Protestant, and Jewish. All who came to America, as far as I know, were Jews. My first Sulzberger ancestor arrived after the 1848 revolution in Germany. But earlier ancestors would have been of greater interest to Christopher. These came in the late seventeenth century from Holland, and were called Haas (or hare), the animal he is bred to chase. My forebear built a boat with his brothers, loaded it with family and dogs, and sailed over the Atlantic: farmers all. Christopher himself is of English ancestry from Lincolnshire, where he was born. He converted to Greek Orthodoxy. I venture he is the only Greek Orthodox beagle from Lincolnshire now alive, although his late predecessor, Benjamin, shared that distinction in his day.

I finally got off the autoroute at Baden-Baden, miles from where I wanted to be, in black darkness. I inquired the way of one person after another but find that many Rhineland Germans speak as if they have a mouthful of mashed potatoes. Finally I came across a willing enough young man who looked exactly like Danny Kaye and who spoke like Danny Kaye imitating a nervous Rhineland German youth. He kept twitching as he spoke, each twitch making him still more nervous. And he kept saying in every sentence that I must go under, not over, the Basel-Frankfurt Autobahn.

There was no other autobahn around. Finally, found a road to a ferry, waited at the port until the little ship showed up, and crossed at a village named Rüdesheim. Drove on to Brumath, a French village north of Strasbourg, where a charming Hostellerie à l'Ecrevisse took us in. It was on a small stream called La Zorn which contained pike and carp. The landlady, nice as pie, told me that Brumath was once a Roman town.

In the morning we rode to Colmar and stopped at the wonderful museum where Matthias Grünewald's great paintings are. The museum is in the old (1252) convent of Unterlinden, built while some people still knew Colmar as Columbaria. The nuns were dispossessed by the Revolution in 1790 but an artistic society was started in 1847 and from this the museum derived. It is very catholic, including modern works by Monet, Renoir, Rouault, Léger, and Picasso, as well as Vasarely and Poliakoff, but its great treasures are the fifteenth-century paintings of Matthias Grünewald and Martin Schongauer. Schongauer was born in Colmar and Grünewald in Würzburg. He painted the famous altarpiece of Issenheim at a convent there and this is displayed at Colmar, one of the ten free cities of Alsace in the fifteenth century.

Then off again for Colombey-les-Deux-Églises, stopping first at Langres to lunch in its ancient Hôtel du Cheval Blanc, another church property dispossessed by the Revolution. Colombey, on a slight rise in rolling country, is easily identified from afar by a huge granite Croix de Lorraine (de Gaulle's personal sign for the Liberation movement) set atop a hill beside his country residence. This is the cross Churchill told Roosevelt was the heaviest he had to bear. Christopher and I walked up the woodland path leading to it, then around it, then went to the little cemetery of the village church where de Gaulle's grave, under a high ordinary cross, bears inscribed tributes from liberated prisoners and other organizations.

The general's estate is modest, not of great extent, and bounded by low brick walls and a closed gate. There is no hint of its former occupant except a "private property" sign. I thought it was proper that Christopher should do homage since de Gaulle, who didn't like many humans, did like dogs. Time after time his Alsatian would climb on the bed and when Madame de Gaulle remonstrated, "Charles, Charles, do something," he would say, "Yes, dear" — and the dog would remain.

 We were in Paris exactly one month. I was entirely occupied with replacing my marvelous secretary, Linda Lamarche, a loyal and dear friend who had been offered another far better paid job which I, in my retirement, could not hope to match. So Linda helped me as I interviewed one after another possibility, finally settling on an English girl who turned out to be a lemon.

Despite the absence of rippling, somewhat summer-parched grass, the piney smells, the occasional clumps of flowers, the scent of citrus trees, and the lapping, clear blue sea, Christopher was quite delighted to get back to Paris, the city he likes best. It has been blatantly plain to him from the days of his early puppyhood that the French adore dogs.

During his brief sojourn Christopher reacquainted his not-too-fastidious palate with the taste of Gallic cooking; frequented some of his favorite spots, including the British embassy garden, rendered especially juicy because of the habit of Zorba, the ambassadorial dalmatian, of burying his bones in secret nooks only discoverable to talented, four-legged sniffers; and called on various two-legged personal friends.

On September 28, 1978 we took off again. Christopher was as

eager as ever to get back to his usual nest on the floor before the front seat of the car he so detested. Our target was Chambéry in Savoy, where we spent our first night en route back to Greece, with loads of books, manuscripts, my electric typewriter, and so forth. Chambéry is an old town, beautifully set in the Alpine foothills, and surrounded by green fields and woodstreams — lovely country. It was once the capital of the duchy of Savoy and only became a permanent part of France in the nineteenth century. The château of the dukes, part of which dates back to the fourteenth century, is an impressive, pleasing mixture of jumbled styles. One of the main monuments in town is the Fountain of the Elephants, erected in memory of Count Benedicto de Boigne (1751–1820) who made a fortune in India serving the Mahratta ruler.

Christopher and I took several walks. He was much impressed by the inhabitants' evident interest in eating: food shops, restaurants, and game shops with huge hanging boars everywhere. Chambéry "looks" more French than Italian but, without any nationalist movement, it is a typical European frontier locale and there is a 1912 statue for those who died for *"la patrie,"* not saying which wars. The people are friendly and civilized; the atmosphere agreeable.

Next day, we drove on through Savoy and Upper Savoy, crossing past Megève, St. Gervais, and Chamonix to enter the Mont Blanc tunnel, longest underground passage in the world (about seven miles). It is a splendid drive and on a fine early autumn day the sun shone brightly and snow gleamed from the mountains ringing Chamonix. Mont Blanc was dazzling but I could not awake any interest in Christopher who ascertains all beauty with his nose or taste buds.

We emerged into the Valle d'Aosta, smallest autonomous region of Italy, at Courmayeur. It is notable that on this side of the border many speak both Italian and French or a kind of Provençal patois. In one valley, Gressoney, a German dialect is spoken.

Aosta used to be inhabited by Celtic-Ligurian tribes who were conquered by a Roman general in 24 B.C. In 1032 it came under the house of Count Umberto, founder of the Savoy dynasty. Aosta itself is an ugly town, jammed with modern, jerrybuilt, ugly blocks of flats, but it contains, hidden away or on its outskirts, some fine old ruins from Roman and medieval days.

We drove to Rimini from Aosta, crossing the nearby Rubicon, now a dried-up brook, beyond which the Roman Senate banned the advance into Rome's territory of any armed soldiers or units bearing standards. How invisible it looks today. Caesar crossed it and marched on Rome in November, 50 B.C.

Christopher was furious to discover that at the excellent hotel where we stayed he was not even allowed in the restaurant. There was a big fuss when I unsuccessfully tried to insist; he barked, growled and showed his teeth. We walked out haughtily and found a pleasant, modest joint.

Rimini was a seat of the Gallic tribe of Sena in the fourth century B.C. The Romans took it in 27 B.C. In the eighth century A.D. it became part of the papal domains in the Romagna; then a free commune in the thirteenth century, finally coming under the suzerainty of the renowned Malatesta family. In the late thirteenth century occurred the famous love affair of Francesca da Rimini and Paolo who were murdered by her husband when discovered in bed together. Giovanni, the husband, was Paolo's brother. Today there is a splendid ruin of the thirteenth-to-fourteenth-century castle of the Malatestas.

The most famous Malatesta was Sigismondo (fifteenth century) for whom the castle is now named. Pope Pius II said Sigismondo was well versed in history and philosophy and able to do anything, but he excommunicated him as "luxury-loving, incestuous, conspiratorial, assassin, fraud, thief, perjurer, liar, counterfeiter, heretic, blasphemer, faithless."

On to Ancona to embark for Patras on the *Mediterranean Sky*, a large and modern Greek ship. We lunched in a hilltop restaurant and then I walked Christopher for miles to get him ready for a thirty-six-hour sea voyage. When we boarded, I was brusquely ordered by shouting officers to put him in the kennel but, after judicious tips to stewards, smuggled him to my cabin and we stayed there, eating only occasional sandwiches and dog biscuits, emerging once each night for a pee. He was even happier than I to reach the ghastly town of Patras and drive on toward Spetsais.

Drinks and dinner with the Kyrous next day. Kyrou means "son of Cyrus" and Adonis's father was named Kyros Kyrou, the equivalent of Cyrus Cyrusson. So apart from liking and respecting him a lot, it gives me, an American Cyrus, a special bond.

We discussed a venture we are engaged in — searching for the underwater remnants of Venetian, Genoese, and Byzantine ships sunk near Spetsopoula in the thirteenth century during a great battle. Stavros Niarchos, who now owns Spetsopoula, is fascinated, having read a column by me on the subject, and is financing the operation. Prime Minister Caramanlis is also personally interested and wants to come down and watch key events. Professor Katzev of the University of Pennsylvania, renowned submarine archaeologist, who raised the fourth-century b.c. ship off Kyrenia, Cyprus, will be in charge of operations, aided by his wife, also an expert. An Italian-made three-man submarine is expected to arrive here by ship and trailer-truck, via Patras, in about three days. Gialouris, head of archaeology for the Greek Ministry of Culture, is part of the group. I had been asked to say nothing about it but with that many Greeks involved the secret will be out in hours. Already there is rivalry among the civil servants in the Ministry of Culture for publicity and the favor of Niarchos.

Two days later Adonis telephoned in despair. The Ministry of Culture is trying to fudge everything up and delay events until the end of the month, when the weather will be too rough for the midget submarine. On October 20 I had drinks with Kyrou and the Katzevs, who came briefly to Spetsais in connection with the project.

They and Adonis are furious with the Greek bureaucracy. The Ministry of Culture has stalled and stalled. Now they are demanding all kinds of new conditions — rather strange when what is at stake is a free ride offered by Niarchos, who is ready to finance the deal alone and build a museum in Spetsais to house its discoveries.

On Saint Barbara's day, December 4, we went to the little church of Saint Barbara on the hillside by the island's convent to attend the christening of the fourteen-month-old daughter of Nikolo, the coachman. The baptismal font had been borrowed from another church. There was only one priest, dressed in dark red, heavy silk, his hair done up in a bun, and a one-man chorus who chanted quite well, without music. The church was almost full with about fifty of Nikolo's friends and family, including lots of children, some of them solemnly chewing gum throughout the service.

Christopher was allowed to peer eagerly through the door and watch. The baby very much disliked being dunked in the font, filled with one jerry-can of hot water, one jerry-can of cold water, and a bottle of olive oil. There was a pathetic censer swinging and faint whiffs of incense. On the whole, touching, pleasing, and very human. Nikolo, who also has three older girls, was very excited although his poor dog, whom he adores, is dying, suffering from some weird, deadly disease known locally as *morva*. Two other dogs have already died of it and I never let Christopher off the leash now, for fear he might catch it from a friend.

December was unpleasant if eventful. For four weeks there were continual rains, strong winds, and biting cold. Since the house had been invaded by workers installing a central heating system, it was like living in the heart of the London blitz. Great holes hacked through the thick, 140-year-old walls to make way for pipes and wires; savage cold all day and night; furniture, debris, plaster, and filth piled all over the place. Then I tripped one night and broke my toe, and have been hobbling rather than let one of the local medical worthies treat me. (I'd end up with an amputation at the hip.)

Driving to Athens for three days of Christmas shopping (Paddy and Joan Leigh Fermor were coming and I needed food and presents), a phenomenal thing happened. It was a rough, windy, rainstormy day. About twenty-five miles along, atop a high pass, I ran into a combined sleet and hail storm. Before I knew quite what was happening, the wind began shoving me across the road — which was sheeted with unexpected ice — although I was only going about forty miles per hour. It lifted me right off, and down I went along a drenched hillside, ending in a newly ploughed field where I was able to halt the car, having prevented it from turning over. Lucky at that. Six feet to my left was a sharp declivity. If I'd gone over that, I'd have been a deader. This was not the "well-crafted" death I had in mind.

Final disaster: the *morva* seems to be a fatal malady called kala-azar and dogs are dying all over the island — including several of Christopher's friends.

Nevertheless, a very pleasant Christmas. The central heating system was finally finished late December 23, just after I had brought guests over by boat from the mainland. Christmas, with turkey, plum pudding, and lots of booze, cheered everyone up. Paddy and Joan are charming and intelligent. Paddy was commander of the operation under which Britain's SOE landed two men in Nazi-occupied Crete and captured General Kreipe, the German commander in chief, taking him off to Cairo. Paddy liked him a lot. Kreipe was an ardent classicist and later told a German TV audience that Paddy had behaved like a knight and in a most chivalrous fashion. Paddy got a Distinguished Service Order for it. He and Joan now have a lovely house in the Mani where they live all year and he writes very good books.

Also at dinner: Hod Fuller and his Greek wife Dozia, and Jovita, my sweet little Spanish cook. Hod is a retired U.S. Marine

Corps general who was senior American officer in the Jedburgh team operations under which small British and American groups were parachuted into France to spur on the resistance and hinder the Germans. There is a Place Colonel Fuller in the town of Royan, near Bordeaux.

Nineteen seventy-nine was ushered in by Epiphany, January 6 — sunny, warm. This is one of the year's great holidays. I sat in the *dapia* (main square) which was jammed with the entire island population and visitors from the mainland, all dolled up in their Sunday best. A small religious parade wound through the crowd as boat horns blew and cats, undisturbed by the occasion, stretched sleepily under tables or in sunny, protected corners. The principal churches of the dozens dotted about Spetsais echoed with chants.

The procession through the *dapia* was led by choirboys bearing banners and unlit old lamps on poles, followed by singing cantors and the island's three priests, bearded, wearing black cylindrical "pope's" hats and golden-colored long robes. Both moving and merry. The day's mood changed rapidly later. A great wind came up, chilling the air and churning huge waves: real winter once again. Communications with the mainland vanished.

In front of the large house behind the *dapia* is the home of Sotiriou Anargyrou, great benefactor of Spetsais, a self-made millionaire who returned here from overseas and built the boarding school, Greece's Eton. Just beside that is a bronze bust of the island's heroine, Admiral Laskarina Bouboulina, the lady who fought the Turks during the Independence War. Nearby, I pointed out to Christopher a small marble plaque at the base of a little photographer's shop. It says in French:

Here from 1827 to 1832 were preserved in a barrel of rum the mortal remains of Paul Marie Bonaparte, nephew of Napoleon I, emperor of the French, who offered his life for the independence of Greece, 1809–1827. Gift of Monsieur

Guy Picat, Philhellene of Paris, to the Church of St. Nicolas of Spetsai, May 1975.

Afterwards we strolled through the rain to the lighthouse on the point, where Christopher decided to take a swim. On the way back, going through the boatyard where builders were slowly hacking away at the orange-painted frames of various-sized barks and caiques, I observed that the only visible difference in boat building since Homeric times is that nowadays the buzz saw cuts the wood, and iron nails instead of wooden pegs hold the boards and keel together.

Christopher and I visited the little museum January 15. It is in the family mansion of Hadziyannis Mexis, first archon of Spetsais. It's a handsome, tall building of only two steep stories, the upper one of which boasts a graceful, cloisterlike arched balcony. Below is a garden which, in the winter sun, is lovely: flowers and blossoming almond trees. In one corner, and outside the gate, are two huge sailing-ship's anchors, each a good rusty ten feet long. In the courtyard in front are busts of Bouboulina, and of ten befezzed male revolutionary colleagues of the 1821 Independence War.

The mansion is quite a bit above and east of the *dapia,* where the main cannon battery was then deployed and which is now the haven of tourists and café-idlers. At the time of the revolt, the bishop's seat was in the Church of the Assumption and was monastic. Napoleon's nephew occupied one of the cells. The chapel on the old harbor, where I live, is called Panayia Armadas and commemorates an 1822 naval victory over the Turks which is still celebrated each September with fireworks and the burning of a "Turkish ship." The nunnery behind and well above the harbor is called Ahioi Pendes. Spetsais was called Pityoussa in ancient times, meaning "pine tree island." It was the first of the archipelago to revolt against the Turks, in April, 1821, and Spetsiot sailors were famed for their ferocity.

X   Arrived in Brindisi late the afternoon of January 18, 1979 en route to Paris in my excellent Volkswagen Passat, accompanied by Jovita and Christopher. We had left Spetsais that morning, closing the house down, locking it, and giving the keys to the gardener; and had rocked across to Costa on the mainland in the little bark *Atromitos.*

First, we visited Epidaurus, which Jovita had never seen, and I gave her a guided tour. The ancient sanctuary of Epidaurus was like a classical Baden-Baden with extras — a sanctuary of Asclepios, the Greek god of medicine, and also a fashionable resort. Asclepios himself derived from the old Egyptian statesman-god, Imhotep, who lived around 2780 B.C., making Asclepios much nearer to us in time than to his predecessor. Imhotep was a kind of pharaonic prime minister and his tomb at Sakkara, near Cairo, is fully excavated and lovely.

Epidaurus was at the height of its fame during the fourth century B.C. and had various "cure" facilities, homes of priest-physicians, hospitals, sanitoria, hotels, sporting fields, baths, and amusements for the healthy. Every four years a dramatic festival was held there nine days after the games at nearby Isthmia. It was so renowned internationally that the Romans, in the third century B.C., sent for the sacred serpent of Epidaurus to stamp out an epidemic.

The whole complex of buildings was excavated about ninety years ago by Mary Henderson's grandfather, Professor Cavaddias. The theater, now used every summer, is the best preserved of Greece's antique theaters, has magnificent acoustics and holds an audience of fourteen thousand. The old seats of honor were in red limestone, the others in white. The original temple had doors of ivory and contained a gold and ivory statue of Asclepios seated on a throne, a staff in one hand, the head of a serpent in the other, a dog crouched by his side, just as I had one crouched by mine as I explained all this.

I had a hard time figuring out a one-day itinerary for Jovita that would still get us to our boat at Patras in time. The Peloponnesos is famous for its beauty. The area has been inhabited since the third millennium B.C. and many place names, like Mycenae and Corinth, seem to be of Asiatic origin. Its first inhabitants used copper even before bronze was mixed. In the second millennium B.C. Greek-speakers came in and eventually founded the warlike Mycenaean civilization with its heroic traditions of Perseus and Hercules.

After Philip of Macedon was elected leader of the Hellenic world, Corinth became the historical center of the Peloponnesos until, in the feudal wars of the Franks and crumbling Byzantium, Monemvasia was regained by the Byzantine emperor Michael III Paleologus. After that, confusion reigned: intramural Frankish wars, Slavs, Turks, Albanians, until 1821 when Archbishop Germanos of Patras raised a revolt.

In Isthmia, we lunched on what Christopher assures me are the best souvlakia in Greece. Then we drove on to Corinth and its famous mountain citadel of Acrocorinth, which protected the ancient commercial center below it, linking Europe and Asia long before the canal was cut. In classical days Corinth is said to have contained 300,000 citizens and as many as 460,000 slaves; now it has a population of less than 40,000.

Its ancient inhabitants worshipped Aphrodite and were notorious for their vices, even in vicious times. Saint Paul spent eighteen months there and commented: "Evil communications corrupt good manners." Corinth served as the main Greek headquarters in the major battles of the Persian War. It was linked by long walls running from Acrocorinth to the seacoast of the gulf.

Acrocorinth is still so formidable looking that one cannot understand how it fell successively to Byzantine, Frankish, Venetian, and Turkish armies. The day was cold, windy, grey, and beautiful. The great limestone mountain, rising almost 1,900 feet from the plain below, looks (as it was long thought to be) like one of Europe's strongest natural fortresses. It is a steep drive up a rutted dirt road and an even steeper climb from there to the first set of walls, over an old dry moat which once was spanned by a drawbridge. The higher of its two summits, backed by natural rock, once contained a Temple of Aphrodite, whose worship was aided by a thousand holy courtesans. Alas, those days are gone. The view is tremendous, either with clouds roaring overhead or a gleaming look into the distance as far as Aegina, Athens, and Naupactos.

We finally took off for Patras and our boat. The trip to Brindisi (a night and day) was uneventful save for the usual game of hiding Christopher under blankets whenever a wary crew searched for him to put him in the dog-cage section. As usual we won. He plays the game well; doesn't stir or make a sound. After arriving, I took him and Jovita to the famous piazza where the Appian Way ended (to restart in Albania) and where Virgil lived at the moment of his death: a splendid site.

Long drive across Italy and France penetrating snowstorms, sleet, hail, rain, and fog. A miserable trip — so bad that whenever I stopped to water or walk Christopher, he didn't even want to get out of the car. Livorno, where we spent one night, is really a lovely port city, with scarcely anything remaining from earlier days when it was overshadowed by Pisa and, of course, Genoa. The hotel was splendid. Jovita and I each had an enormous room which, to save money, was without bath; but since the hotel was nearly empty, the floor bath was ours.

I took Christopher down to the bar after a brief stroll along the icy waterfront. Two old, old men, looking like characters out of a nineteenth-century novel and gloomily dressed in that style, were sitting alone, pale and white. One was reading aloud to the other, whose lips silently formed sounds and words as they went along. I thought he was blind until, after the first man left, he picked up a paper and clearly was perusing it. I suspect the departed man was an employee, hired to read to his boss.

Finally, after almost eight hundred kilometers through an endless series of tunnels and a winding road, I decided we'd stop at Montélimar, well up the Rhône valley, because a great bank of evening fog was looming just ahead. We got rooms at the Relais de l'Empereur, a charming, comfortable, if very touristy, hotel. Montélimar boasts it is the world's nougat capital. The barman explained that in the nineteenth century there was an old lady who made the candy for her grandchildren and they used to say: "*Grandmère, nous gatte,*" and that this is where the word "nougat" comes from. As good a tale as any.

The hotel was started in the eighteenth century as the Relais de la Poste and on April 24, 1814, Napoleon and his guards spent the night there on the way to exile in Elba. He had previously visited the Relais in 1793, 1795, and on returning from his disastrous Egyptian campaign in 1799. In 1830, it was decided to exploit the Napoleonic connection; the name was changed and the start of a collection of Napoleonic relics begun. This is now scattered about the various salons and stairways.

Arrived back in Paris after a foggy, foggy journey.

One February afternoon, Christopher and I walked over to the house of Princess Olga for a quiet cup of tea. I brought my book on Marina. The princess looked very well and lovely although she is now approaching eighty. Her style of life has certainly changed since Prince Paul died over a year ago. She lives modestly and opened the door herself because, as she explained, her manservant is a bit deaf so she had come downstairs and done the job. She has sold her car and now takes the bus everywhere. She spent Christmas all alone because, although she had been invited to Versailles, there were to be more than twenty other people there and she thought Christmas should be with the family and a few close friends and if not that, alone.

We sat and chatted in a tiny little television room set off from the sitting room, where Christopher, as usual, distinguished himself by stealing a cookie from the box — fortunately the last one — while we were talking and not noticing. But he was stupid enough to leave crumbs all over the floor which called our attention to his misdemeanor.

Princess Olga talked a lot about the Greek royal family to which she is connected. Her father was Prince Nicholas, a brother of King Constantine I. She said that ex-Queen Frederika now lives in India near Madras in a comfortable house with six servants. She has snow-white hair and wrinkled brown skin, "just like the other Indians," and wears saris but adorns herself with huge quantities of jewels. She is very fond of her grandchildren and goes to Spain often to see her daughter, Queen Sophia, and the kids.

At noon one March day, Christopher and I walked over to Philippe de Rothschild's on the rue Méchain, very near the Paris Observatory. We were greeted by Philippe and his seven-year-old golden Labrador, Rajah. It is a charming small house, filled with exquisite chinoiserie decorated by Pauline, his late wife.

After what he called a "snack," which featured a very good Château Mouton, Philippe told me something about the wine business in France. He said that the present system of rating the Bordeaux wines is based upon a governmental decision made in 1855 during the first Paris Exposition, which featured a visit from Queen Victoria, the first British sovereign to come to France on friendly terms in years. Most of her predecessors had come over as conquerors.

In deciding how to present the clarets, which have for so many generations been favorite drinking among English gentlemen, the government asked the advice of the Bordeaux region growers, brokers, and merchants. By general agreement they decided to divide the vineyards into five categories or *crus* starting with a *premier cru* of four members: Château Lafite, Château Margaux, Château Haut-Brion, and Château Latour. Château Mouton-Rothschild was not included in the *premier cru* listing, primarily as a result of what was tantamount to a blackball by the Château Lafite influence. Lafite was run by another branch of the Rothschild family to which Philippe is only distantly related. The original wines of Lafite had been introduced to the court of Louis XIV during the seventeenth century by the Comte de Ségur. Château Mouton, according to this decision, was made number one in the listing of the *deuxième cru*. According to Philippe, it was a kind of "two-and-a-half" or "two plus" and in between "one" and "two."

As for the others — second, third, fourth, and fifth categories — they have been stuck with their ratings ever since, although a wine like Château Cantemerle, listed in the *cinquième cru*, is frequently a superior wine to all the others except perhaps a *premier cru*. These five listings apply above all to the wines of the Médoc. Pauillac is more of an appellation than a geographical district. As for "Bordeaux" as a name, it includes any wine that has been grown in Bordeaux and really is only a designation, not a guarantee that the wine is good. Philippe was put in charge of the Château Mouton vineyard in 1922, when he was twenty years old. It had originally been brought into the family by his grandfather, one of the English Rothschilds.

At the time Philippe took control, he knew nothing at all about wines. The only people, in fact, who did know about the splendid leading wines of Bordeaux were the old peasant families who had been growing them for years and years. Philippe himself was just a youngster who was fond of auto racing and, indeed, took part in the Le Mans Grand Prix in a Stutz Bearcat.

But he worked hard and within six months knew a great deal. From then on he tried desperately to get the rating of Mouton included in the *premier cru*, raising the list to five. But he was continually blocked by his distant cousin Elie de Rothschild, who from 1947 on was in charge of the Château Lafite operation. He claims Elie played a great many dirty tricks on him in order to keep him out. Philippe was only able to get Mouton included in the top rating in 1975.

Philippe invented the idea of having wines "bottled at the Château." Prior to that, the only wines bottled at the château were a relatively few bottles to be used by the owner and his family and friends. The rest was sent in barrels to merchants in Bordeaux who took care of the bottling and selling. In the seventeenth century, when the great wines of Bordeaux first became widely known, they were always put in barrels when harvested and were sold by the barrel to the court or to the grandees who purchased them. Then they were drawn out of the barrel by the purchaser when and as desired.

March 19 Christopher and I gave a tiny farewell party for Nicko and Mary Henderson at Lucas Carton, the second time I'd been there since I retired on December 31, 1977. Present were the two Hendersons and Christopher, the greatest admirer of the Lucas cuisine. He had been starved at lunch to prepare him for the event. Derry and Alexandra (Henderson) Moore joined us at the table after dinner and descended with us to the *cave*.

It was a sad occasion. The Hendersons leave for good April 1. He is retiring; British regulations say when an ambassador reaches sixty, he's out. (He was later called out of retirement and sent to Washington.) And I leave shortly so they won't be here when I return. Will Christopher and I ever see them again? I haven't felt so sad about the departure of friends since U.S. ambassador Chip Bohlen and his wife, Avis, left.

Christopher ate his dinner with dazzling speed. I permitted him to have a second portion, in honor of the occasion. He then accompanied us to the *cave* where he sniffed some very fine odors such as jeroboams of Lafite and ancient cognacs. Also, Madame Allegrier, widow of my old friend Alex, the previous *patron*, had prepared a special cake decorated with the French and British flags. Christopher consumed more than the Hendersons. Alas, I fear that for all but him, the evening was a flop.

Dined informally one night at Alain and Mary de Rothschild's with Christopher — who amazed everyone, including me, by his good behavior. The main feature of the evening, as far as I was concerned, was a 1945 Château Lafite — in ample quantities. Christopher was not served this delicious wine.

Indeed, it was not his best stay in Paris. I took the little fellow repeatedly to the U.S. embassy residence where he was to marry Abigail Hartman, a not-quite-two-year-old beagle bitch. After a series of failures we had to keep a schedule and take off for Belgrade.

The trouble was she just wasn't quite in heat. They gamboled merrily across the huge embassy lawn and in and out of flowers. But no sex. And each day ended in drenching downpours of cold showers that ruined even their pleasant platonic games. I hoped for better results on Christopher's return.

We left April 28 for Duingt, France. Fifty-odd years ago I had spent a couple of summer holidays there on the Lac d'Annecy and adored it so I decided to make this our first stop as Christopher began a new pilgrimage to Spetsais. I don't believe you can communicate personal memories to dogs but I am convinced that he, too, liked it. And Duingt has changed comparatively little when seen against a world backdrop. Of course, the huge and gentle old Saint Bernard dog I admired so much as a nine or ten-year-old had long since gone to some pleasant paradise. But there were still ducks and swans swimming placidly on the cold, deep, slate-grey waters of the lake and it remains a thrill to watch a swan flying low and heavy over the water below the snow-dusted, cloud-covered mountains.

The château on a tiny peninsula is still there. It seems to have been somewhat restored, including the tower which so much impressed me because there, through a trapdoor before the medieval lord's throne room, disliked prisoners were dropped to their deaths in a cold, stone-walled pool below.

After dinner, following our long drive from Paris, I took Christopher to see those sights and also to the other château, a bit inland, located on a tiny, rushing trout stream: a heavy, well-proportioned, grey, cubic structure.

Christopher was fascinated when, at the end of a pier, a swan silently glided right up to him. When the bird was only a foot away, he turned and fled in terror, his tail hanging down. We continued our walk inland both (I hope) thinking of Marina as we wandered in the cold, wet spring beneath flowering fruit trees, amid clumps of wild flowers and herds of placid sheep with frolicking lambs.

I guess in one's dotage, one revisits one's youth, so I brought Christopher on to Chamonix for our second stop. I'd reserved ahead because this is a long weekend in France, Tuesday, May first being a national holiday as well as Marina's birthday, and roads and hotels were jammed.

We drove away from the steep Dents du Midi and over a rising valley to the gorge of the Arly River. Through the ski country around Megève and St. Gervais, and past les Contamines where, when that resort had just opened, Marina and I spent a quiet ski holiday without the children in the early 1950s.

Chamonix is a place I visited once in the late 1950s with Marina, the children, and our Greek friends the Averofs. I also holidayed there with my mother when I was about sixteen, enjoying the place thoroughly, playing in hotel tennis tournaments, and becoming enamored of the female half of the professional dancing team at the hotel where we stayed.

To my astonishment, after an entire April marked by fog, cold, sleet, and rain throughout France, we awoke to a brilliant, sunny Sunday. Mont Blanc was gleaming white. The sun hadn't yet crept into the narrow Chamonix valley of the Arve River.

Again, we entered Italy through the long Mont Blanc tunnel

and rushed on as far as Verona, a city which is an excellent example for dogs and men. The former, as Christopher discovered to his delight, can sniff twenty-six centuries in one breath: history at a single gulp, as it were. To the latter, it demonstrates how Italy has been able to enrich its own (and world) culture and survive internal and external destruction. It has lost all wars since the early Caesars; but it has won *the* one war, of survival, just as it has learned how to exist without government.

Had an excellent lunch on the Piazza Bra with Veronese specialties including Valpolicella wine and *stracotto con amarone*, a sort of wine-soaked pot roast with cornmeal mush (like Rumanian *mamaliga*). Then started three hours of sightseeing with a bedraggled Christopher, commencing in the Bra (once a field called Braida). In the piazza, with its crenellated medieval wall, is a first-century B.C. Roman arena which holds twenty-two thousand spectators and is second in size only to Rome's Colosseum. As in all Italy, every stone has been used and reused to build new buildings that are now old.

After the arena had been well-scented by Christopher, we walked on to the old brick house said to have been that of Julietta Capulet, Shakespeare's heroine. He took the story from a sixteenth-century novel by Luigi da Porto. Her real name supposedly, Cappreletti; his, Romeo Montecchi. A nice old brick house with a high stone balcony on which tourists crowded to be photographed.

Returning to the old town to examine the *duomo* (cathedral), I found a plaque in an agreeable stucco house commemorating Giuseppe Zambini, who died there July 25, 1846: *"Inventore dell Elettro Motore Perpetuo."* He should be exhumed. Today's energy crisis requires his "perpetual" secret.

The cathedral is gothic, large, cool, dark, and becandled in front with lovely Venetian columns based on lions' backs. Then strolled across a moated drawbridge into the lovely striated thirteenth-century palace of the della Scala family under whom

Verona was at its peak, and who had Giotto as their guest and gave Dante political refuge. On the walls leading to the della Scala bridge across the Adige were heavy growths of wisteria.

A lovely city: founded in the sixth century B.C., occupied by the Romans, the Gauls, the Ostrogoths, the Lombards, Charlemagne, the Bavarians, Venice, the Habsburgs, and even Napoleon. And here it is, still intact, in its own scarred way, with its own personality.

Had hoped to drive through to Zagreb but my car developed problems that needed checking before Jugoslav mechanics got their noses into it. So we holed up in Trieste, which brought back more fond memories.

Trieste is an example of the splendor of empires, both ancient and modern. Empires were made by soldiers but maintained by imaginative civilians. In this case, the Romans were the first to contribute, the Habsburg Austro-Hungarians the last. It was considered a privilege and a matter of pride to be a citizen of the Roman Empire; and, for a brief time, of the British, French, and Spanish, before that privilege turned to nothing.

I noted that Verona symbolizes the Italians' ability to survive all disasters, including those they manufacture. Trieste, which has in fact politically been Italian only since World War I, demonstrates that now the "idea of Europe" has been revived, each "European" should at least wish for a "European" money which he can save, although nationalism outweighs the reality of a "European" passport or other token of internationalism.

I remember well the squabbles between Latin and Slav as to who would inherit the free territory of Trieste temporarily created in 1945 by the Allied armies: Italy or Jugoslavia. The sky used to fill with brickbats till Trieste seemed darkened like Crécy under its arrows — except for the siesta period when everything calmed down after lunch. In the city's complex history, what could more easily be shrugged off than that spasmodic moment?

There is no longer any Habsburg imperial hinterland for the

great port to serve, nor any transatlantic shipping lines. But Trieste doesn't appear ossified; ships busily unload in the harbor and there is a large tourist and consumer trade, much of it from the Marxist heretic, Jugoslavia.

It seems hard to believe that the argument between Belgrade and Rome kept the world on the edge of conflict for some five years after World War II ended. Who on earth really cared what became of Trieste? One certainly wonders now, on this crowded, busy May Day weekend with people busily enjoying themselves and not a seat in any restaurant or café.

Christopher and I took a walk after lunch. There are remnants in Trieste of almost all periods, from the column in the Piazza Unita near the port, honoring Charles VI, the Habsburg emperor who in 1718 declared it a free port; to the lovely little Roman theater of the second century A.D. and the Roman arch, called the Arch of Richard in honor of the Lion-Hearted, who is said to have visited on his way home from the Crusades.

The cathedral of San Giusto on its hill links eleventh-to-fourteenth-century edifices. It is protected by a fifteenth-century Venetian fortified castle. On the way with Christopher I noted a plaque on the side of a hillside house: "Here I wrote the first episode of my new novel *Ulysses* June 16, 1915." By James Joyce, whose brother, Stanislaus, I once knew here.

San Giusto is a lovely Romanesque edifice with graceful painted arches and spacious internal reaches. Below it is a park decorated with rough stones honoring Trieste's various dead heroes of World War II.

Bursa, the stock exchange, has a fine square, recalling the days when it had a great Habsburg function; and there is an Orthodox Church on the Piazza San Antonio Nuovo, leading to the waterfront, where Slavs and Greek merchants used to worship.

Once again I wondered whether Christopher learns any special thing from his travels. He must, above all in Italy, have absorbed some hint of the continuity of life and enduring smells.

Greece has ancient smells but not continuous ones, as does this land of uninterrupted vitality. There are great gaps in Greece between the scent of oxen roasted by Agamemnon's warriors or the infantry of Pericles and today's largely Turkish cuisine; whereas in Italy there is a strange persistence from the dog-pleasing odor of slaves being fed to lampreys by Nero, the human sacrifices of the Colosseum, and today's street vendors and garlic-spiced dishes of the sea.

Arrived in Belgrade from Trieste after perhaps the most miserable drive in my life. It was a big holiday in Jugoslavia with thousands of cars out and all garages closed. And my car was busted, limping all the way.

Our first day there, we spent eight and a half hours with Milovan Djilas, first talking at his house, then lunching with him and Stephanie (delicious meal as always), then going for a two-and-a-half hour walk. Stephanie and their devoted cook, Mica, vied with each other in feeding and spoiling Christopher as I talked with Milovan. Afterward he had a splendid stroll along the banks of the Danube and Sava, smelling Illyrian, Roman, Serbian, Turkish, Hungarian, Austrian, and Jugoslav fragrances in the ancient battlefield below the walls, while I chatted more with Milovan. They are upset that Aleksa, their twenty-six-year-old son, who is about to go to London School of Economics for a Ph.D., and is now doing his military service, is being badly treated in the army, assigned to menial jobs in a disciplinary unit (obviously because of his father, a renowned dissident). Milovan, by the way, says he can't even go fishing with me because in 1954 he was expelled from the Fisherman's Association, as well as the Politburo and the Communist party, and can't get a license.

We had a rambling conversation as we walked down toward the Danube-Sava confluence. Milovan said that not only the younger generation of boys, but also of girls, is much taller than its parents. They call the latter *vitamina,* or vitamin girls. He said the country is suffering from very bad inflation, high prices, and

10 percent unemployment, exclusive of some 800,000-plus Jugoslav workers employed in western Europe. We discussed Eurocommunism at length. He described it as the "modern social-democracy, a social-democracy for modern capitalism, not nineteenth-century capitalism." But he varied this opinion as we trudged along.

He said there are various "Russian nationalisms" today, even more reactionary than that of Solzhenitsyn who, he agrees, wrote one fine book, *A Day in the Life of Ivan Denisovitch* and, for the rest, was a brave survivor and indomitable enemy of Stalinism. Shcharansky typifies one of these "Russian nationalisms," as distinct from Ukrainian, etc. Wildly anti-Semitic, Shcharansky wishes to blend Soviet power and Russian Orthodox Christianity using the result to "Christianize" the world in terms of Sovietism. It is interesting that his works are being published in Moscow.

All "Russian nationalisms" are anti-Western. They consider the West evil and rotten. Solzhenitsyn in this respect has more influence on the Soviet *apparat* than the scientist Sakharov, who is "westernized." The "Russian nationalists" have far more influence on Soviet society than any western "democratic" influences. People like Shcharansky only criticize Stalinism's brutality as it hampers Russia's messianic role.

Djilas admits he has been an "ideological and intellectual critic" of the system. To some degree Sakharov has played that role in Russia. Trotsky did not, ever. He was anti-Stalin primarily because he was personally embittered.

Stalin, I observed, was a man without adjectives; plain, simple, abrupt. Djilas thought him a great man, horrible as he was; "perhaps greater than Lenin." His basic work, the *Foundations of Leninism,* published in 1924 from a series of speeches, just after Lenin's death, is as important as Marx's *Communist Manifesto.* Today Stalin is underestimated as a theoretician. But after Marx, theory was no longer important; only practice.

Djilas dined with Stalin twice. First in 1944, when he headed

Tito's first military mission to Moscow, seeking aid. He didn't expect to see Stalin and had only requested an interview with Molotov, accompanied by Jugoslav lieutenant general Terzić. He had just finished a lecture to the All-Slav Committee in Moscow when an NKVD lieutenant colonel came up to him and whispered: "You must wind up and come."

Djilas, in his general's uniform, asked: "Where are we going?"

"To see Comrade Stalin."

Djilas interjected: "But we have presents for him. I must go and get them." They had brought simple things like a gun and peasant clothes.

"Don't worry," said the lieutenant colonel, "everything's already in the Kremlin."

Djilas was struck by Stalin's small stature, short body, relatively long legs, drooping pants. Molotov was with him as well as an NKVD man Djilas thinks was called Zhdanov. Also, for a few moments at the start, Stalin's secretary, Poskrebyshev.

Stalin shook hands with Djilas. Then Terzić, although he wore no hat, saluted Stalin and clicked his heels like an old royal officer. He announced his name: "Terzić." Stalin replied with a straight face: "Stalin."

He then asked Djilas: "You've been here a while now. How do you like Russia?" (not the "Soviet Union"). Djilas said he was much impressed. Stalin said: "We are not enthusiastic. But we are doing what we can."

On the eve of Djilas's departure, June 5, 1944, he was taken by Molotov to dine at Stalin's dacha at 9:30 P.M. and they stayed until morning. Stalin drank only a little wine but ate enormously, more than Djilas could imagine a small man consuming. Molotov drank more than his boss. They discussed Britain and Stalin indicated that he disliked Churchill yet respected him. It was all very informal: only the three of them plus the NKVD general. No servants. They served themselves from a sideboard littered with silver-covered platters. Djilas said the food was delicious:

Caucasian and Russian dishes. The only other time he dined with Stalin was in 1948, just before Jugoslavia's fight with Russia and the Comintern.

We were staying with Ambassador Larry Eagleburger, a career diplomat and an exceptionally nice young man of great competence. He even more or less jailed his handsome large Rhodesian ridgeback bitch to protect the loud-mouthed Christopher. He had been preparing to invite Djilas for lunch, as I had suggested in a column in 1977, but now Milovan is under personal attack again and Larry doesn't wish to jeopardize relations.

Next day we again went to Milovan's, first for a walk, then dinner. He said the old Serbian warriors always called their dogs "lions." He also told me the tale of Majka Jevrosima, after whom the street on his corner was named. I hope Christopher understood. It is a very romantic story.

Jevrosima was the wife of a great noble in Serbia who was slain in the famous fourteenth-century battle of Kosovo, fighting on the side of Tsar Lazar against the Turks, who won this battle, ending Serbian independence for a long time. Her husband and her seven sons fought together and when the battle finally ended they were found slain in one corner of the bloody field. They had gone to battle on their horses, accompanied by their "lions" and their falcons. All the animals survived but all the men died. Majka (which means mother) Jevrosima went to the battlefield after the sad news of the defeat came in and, one by one, she discovered her sons' and her husband's corpses. All the animals — the horses, the dogs and the falcons — were weeping with sadness, but she was stern and self-contained and not a tear dropped.

When she returned to her castle she was met by her seven daughters-in-law. She told them what had happened. All of them burst into tears but she retained full control of herself. However, the next day a large raven flew over from Kosovo and dropped a human hand beside the castle. Majka Jevrosima picked it up.

She did not recognize it and showed it to her youngest daughter-in-law, asking if she knew whose hand it was. The girl started weeping and said it was her husband's; she recognized it by the ring. That was too much for the stony-nerved Jevrosima. She dropped dead. The poem goes on, as recounted by guzlars generation after generation, with a prayer that Jevrosima had gone to heaven and there been given by God a pair of swan's wings and the talons of an eagle so she could fly to Kosovo to see again the scene where her family perished.

Our conversation was scattered. Milovan told me about a battle in World War I at Kolubara in northwest Serbia, about forty-five miles from Belgrade. It took place in November 1914 and was one of the decisive battles of a very bad period of the war when the French were striving to hold the Germans back from Paris on the River Marne. At Kolubara the Serbs won a tremendous victory over the Austro-Hungarian army and took seventy thousand prisoners. Incidentally, Djilas said, it was almost a civil war because 49 percent of the Austro-Hungarian soldiers fighting against the Serbs were Croats, their fellow south Slavs. Croatia is now one of the seven republics of the Jugoslav republic.

This reminiscence led Djilas to speculate about Tito himself. Tito, as everyone knows, was a soldier in the Austro-Hungarian army during World War I, was captured by the Russians, and was in a Russian prisoner of war camp when the Bolshevik Revolution came. That is when he openly joined the Communist movement. Djilas wondered if he had voluntarily enlisted in the Austro-Hungarian army in order to seek a career or whether he had been a conscript. He was clearly an ambitious man whose destiny lay far beyond the small Croatian village in which he had been born. Djilas suspects he volunteered. Tito once told Djilas that he was a very avid fencer while he was a soldier. He was ranked as the second best fencer in the entire army and he always resented that he was not acknowledged as the first, the very best. He used to say to Djilas, "I would have been first if I had not been a Croat." That was Tito's way of recollecting that the Croats were not really first-class citizens under the old Habsburg Empire.

Djilas said Stalin's mother was invited by the Soviet dictator to the Kremlin a few years before his death. Stalin never talked about his father, who had been a drunkard and died in abject poverty of alcoholism. But he had an affectionate relationship with his mother. When she came to Moscow and saw the Kremlin she was not enormously impressed. Stalin himself told Djilas, "She said she was sorry that I hadn't finished the theological seminary in Georgia" where he had studied as a boy.

Djilas said Tito has four separate sources of power in Jugoslavia. He runs the army personally. He runs the Party personally. He runs the police personally. And he runs the security guards personally. The security guards are a kind of separate force like the private army of the Soviet Secret Police, which has its own tanks and planes. The Jugoslav security guard does not have aircraft however.

Djilas said Tito, during his days in the Soviet Union as a young Communist, had a very close relationship with the NKVD. It was probably because of this connection that he succeeded as head of the secret, underground Jugoslav Communist party when the previous leadership headed by Milan Gorkić was purged by Stalin.

We then went to Milovan's very nice apartment — modest but comfortable, the walls hung with Jugoslav paintings — and stayed for dinner and postprandial drinks. We also discussed at length a project for going fishing together in Jugoslavia during July.

Milovan is dubious as to whether he could get a license to fish without again becoming a member of the Fisherman's Association — which he thinks is clearly impossible. However, we speculated about the idea. He would like to bring a young relative along because the country is pretty rough and it would be desirable to have a youth to aid two aging gentlemen up and down the canyons. He also said we would have to bring several syringes of snakebite serum because there are quite a few adders in the region during July.

I then wanted to get back to Eurocommunism, which we discussed at length again. He said western politicians think of Eurocommunism only as a reaction to Stalinism in the Soviet system. But an essential reason for the new phenomenon is the existence of democratic western societies whose tolerant openness is more and more familiar to eastern Europe thanks to modern communications. And of course such open western societies tolerate Communist parties, and the local Communist parties in western countries clearly must make concessions in the direction of democracy to attract any kind of following.

This is a very special era which is not generally recognized. It is the first time in history that the basic problems of existence have been solved — food, education, housing. The Soviet type of political system has been outdated by the societies which have accomplished fundamental progress for all people.

The fact of this development of western societies was less clear in the period between the two world wars. Many then thought that the Soviet system would also evolve by its own means. Some intelligent people foresaw that indeed it would become the leader of humanity in its future course — people like André Malraux, Sidney and Beatrice Webb, and George Bernard Shaw. But now those whose liberal instincts were at first impressed, know they were wrong; that the Soviet system is not going to evolve. In fact the legacy of the USSR today weighs heavily in terms of Soviet imperialism, as does the legacy of Stalin's crimes.

And all communism has become more nationalistic, even those Communist parties not controlled by the Soviet line. History since World War II has demonstrated that a Communist party is only internationally-minded until it gains power. Once it gains power in its own country it becomes very nationalistic —

just as the Soviet party has become. No theoretician before World War II could possibly have predicted wars between Communist states like China, Vietnam, and Cambodia. These things — this type of war — are caused by international reasons as well as internal reasons.

At the same time, today modern capitalism is not far from achieving its own form of democratic revolution. I asked Djilas to elaborate on what he had been saying the previous day about the lack of any Marxist philosopher since Karl Marx himself. After all, wasn't a man like Lenin or Mao an important philosopher? He replied that Lenin was a great political polemicist and organizer, but he was not a philosopher. He was a brilliant operator in the struggle for power. His greatest achievement was to invent a new kind of party and to use that party in order to take power. As a matter of fact, in terms of what you might call party philosophy, Stalin's book, *Problems of Leninism,* is the most important work since the Bolshevik Revolution. That and his *Short Course* are really quite brilliant.

I asked him if he agrees that, although Tito was the first successful Eurocommunist, by becoming a Eurocommunist he made a revolt of Eurocommunism within Eurocommunism inevitable. In other words, the victory of Tito over Stalin more or less made inevitable the heresy of Djilas. Djilas admitted, "Eurocommunism became inevitable when Titoism succeeded. National independence caused the heresy, from Moscow's viewpoint, of Titoism. But thereafter Moscow no longer could admit to any difference between me and Tito."

Djilas said the Italian Communists are not clear on any basic questions. They want to have an *Italian* party but they are not entirely clear on their relations with either the Soviet Union or NATO. He said he was speaking in this respect of the Berlinguer faction which now leads the Italian party. Of course one doesn't know if Berlinguer will be able to hold his power or will be overthrown by opposition elements at the top of the Italian party.

He said the Italian party undoubtedly wants to keep some kind of relationship with NATO because it is an "Italian" party and because it fears what might happen in Jugoslavia after Tito's death if Moscow tries to get Jugoslavia forcibly back into a Soviet commonwealth. At the same time it isn't entirely clear about what its actual stand toward the Soviet Union should be.

As for Carrillo, head of the Spanish Communist party, what he is in fact is a left-socialist revisionist. He isn't really a Communist any more. But the case of Berlinguer is not so clear. The pro-Berlinguer group in Italy is pluralist and would favor several parties in an Italian state. But will they be able to keep control of the party? Djilas thinks they probably will.

Djilas said that Jugoslavia is a curious mixture. In its foreign policy it is certainly independent of the Soviet Union and very committed to its own ideas of a nonaligned block of nations. But internally a good deal of the old authoritarian Soviet tradition still prevails. Nevertheless, at the 1976 Berlin Conference of International Communist Parties, the Jugoslavs had eleven specific points of difference with the Soviets. Djilas admitted Eurocommunists are all in agreement in never mentioning Stalinism. They always mention Marx, however. They rarely mention Leninism anymore.

I asked him, if Karl Marx had been proven right in his prophesies and communism had come to power first in a western industrialized country, didn't he think that Marx himself would have been a Eurocommunist? He said Marx would have foreseen communism as it developed in the Eurocommunist movement. A Karl Marx of today would have been strongly against the Soviet Union.

He said that in eastern Europe all Communist countries have the same power structure but they vary in the degree of freedom accorded to social and human relationships. Also, there are economic differences, such as those between Jugoslavia and Hungary. Poland and Hungary have closer relations with the West. Poland and Jugoslavia are not collectivized in their agriculture.

The role of the Catholic church in Poland is very, very powerful and it is now democratic and progressive. This is a very important development within the Catholic church.

On leaving Jugoslavia the next day I reflected: "The revolution certainly has not helped dogs here now. It takes a lot of wangling, pressure, and bribery to get Christopher into any hotel and no restaurant would dream of having him unless it's an out-of-doors, simple little *kafana*. The lives of humans may have been improved by Marxism but that is certainly not true of the lives of their best friends."

XI   We returned to Greece in early May. It was a hell of a drive to Salonika. Along the way we were menaced by Jugoslav, Greek, and Turkish drivers — none of whom are skilled behind the wheel. There were also just enough slow trucks and occasional horse-drawn vehicles to make the whole thing tedious and dangerous.

We stopped by the roadside for lunch in Titov Veles, which I knew under the name of Veles, before Tito had ever been heard of. It is on the banks of the Vardar (in Greece, Axios) River which flows on down to the Mediterranean near Salonika. At a little joint I ordered two portions of *raznići*. Christopher ate his very greedily and then I gave him mine. By serving him on the floor of the out-of-doors porch, I was able to get away with it. I also provided his own plastic water bowl.

"The last time I was here," I told him, "was in April 1941 when there was a war on. One of the two bridges over the river was down and the other, a railway bridge, was burning. The German bombers had hit both bridges easily. There were no defenses. I drove over the burning railway bridge. That was the only way to get to the other side, to safety. It was the only way, you see."

Christopher said nothing. He regarded me with affectionate disinterest. He licked his muzzle to savor the taste of *raznići*. The *raznići* itself had long since vanished.

At the frontier, the Greek customs officials were, as is their wont, needlessly rude, insolent, and bossy. As soon as a Greek puts on a uniform, he tries to push everybody around. They kept me for about an hour with needless nitpicks.

I had arranged through the Belgrade embassy for the U.S. consulate general in Salonika to reserve a room for me and Christopher. Originally I sought to get accommodation in the hotel Mediterranean Palace because I knew they took dogs. In November 1940, wirehaired fox terrier Felix and I were asleep on the top floor of the Mediterranean Palace when Italian bombers blew it up, knocking us out of bed and wounding Felix. Unfortunately the Mediterranean Palace was under repair and taking no customers; it had been badly shaken in an earthquake.

However the consulate said they would get us equivalent accommodation in the hotel Makedonia Palace. The Makedonia Palace first said there was no reservation at all. I insisted and when they went through their records they found they did have one. But they looked victoriously at Christopher and said, "It doesn't mention dogs. It doesn't say that you have a dog with you. We do not allow dogs in the hotel." Christopher regarded them with a look of stony disinterest. I raved and ranted to no avail. Finally, after one hour, the manager, who had been standing by watching, got them to call up the consulate, who confirmed everything. Then he said that, as a special exception, they would allow the two of us in for the night. A dog's life in the Balkans is not happy.

Shortly after our return to Spetsais, Ewald von Kleist and his lovely wife Gundula came to stay. They are charming and he is especially interesting in terms of the July 20, 1944 plot against Hitler in which he played a very active role. The essential purpose of the plot was to persuade the West to keep the Soviet

Union out of Germany once the conspirators had gotten rid of Hitler and the Nazi system. One evening over drinks, with Christopher stretched before us on the terrace, he recounted his tale.

Admiral Canaris, chief of the German intelligence service, or Abwehr, was not important to the conspiracy itself because he was already declining in power. Indeed, Canaris had actually been dismissed from command of the Abwehr by the time the plot actually exploded. However he had been very useful earlier on. Also he took many of the plotters into the Abwehr under his protection, people like Colonel Hans Oster and Hans von Dohnanyi, a lawyer who eventually became Oster's deputy at the Abwehr.

I asked Ewald what made General Friedrich Fromm, commander of the Home Army, waver so much. He had been on the side of the plotters but then as soon as he learned that Hitler had not died when the bomb went off at headquarters, he shifted his loyalties right back to the führer. Kleist said Fromm was not anti-Nazi. He was simply an opportunist. He saw that the war was being lost and therefore was inclined to be sympathetic to the plotters. His chief of staff was Colonel Klaus Philip Maria, Count von Stauffenberg, the man who placed the bomb in Hitler's headquarters at Rastenburg and was subsequently executed. Stauffenberg gave Fromm the idea that things must be changed in Germany because the war was inevitably lost and a government of non-Nazis could at least salvage something from the wreckage. He implied to Fromm that if the latter played some role in this successful conspiracy it would help Fromm's personal future.

When Stauffenberg flew back to Berlin from Rastenburg, he told Fromm that Hitler was dead and that Fromm should immediately call out the very large Home Army, which was spread all over Europe, and start weeding out Nazis and taking over control of administration and security. But Fromm was very cautious. He called up Hitler's headquarters to find out just exactly what the situation was.

Field Marshal Keitel, who had been present in the führer's headquarters at the time of the explosion, assured Fromm that Hitler was still alive. Kleist and Stauffenberg heard the end of Fromm's conversation and immediately understood that Keitel had told Fromm Hitler wasn't dead.

Stauffenberg said that it was impossible. He expostulated: "I did it myself. I put in that bomb and I saw the explosion."

Fromm replied: "Well he is not dead. You must now shoot yourself. The attempt has failed."

Stauffenberg refused. He said: "I am not going to shoot myself and I don't believe you."

Fromm, who was a tall, very fat man, came out from behind his desk and said: "If that is the case, then I shall arrest you."

Stauffenberg answered: "It is we who will do the arresting, not you." He added to Fromm: "You have just five minutes in which to decide," (meaning on whose side he was, the Nazis' or the plotters').

After five minutes, General Friedrich Olbricht, deputy commander of the Home Army, joined the group in Fromm's office. Fromm told Olbricht: "Under these circumstances I gather I am forced to remain on the sidelines," implying that he would not be an active participant on either side of the fence.

Kleist said: "We put him in a small room and shut him up there. He only asked for one thing — a bottle of brandy."

Later, when it became absolutely clear that Hitler had indeed survived the plot, Fromm emerged and ordered Stauffenberg promptly executed. Stauffenberg and several others who had been rounded up were taken out and shot. Clearly Fromm was trying to eliminate all those who had any idea that he had been connected with the conspiracy.

There was a battalion in Berlin under the command of Major Otto Remer. The plotters were very short on troops because the secret of the conspiracy had to be kept as limited as possible. But they had hoped Remer would use his battalion to encircle those ministries which were the keys to control of the situation. Remer's battalion started off by disarming Hitler's SS Life Guards. Then Remer was ordered to arrest Joseph Goebbels. Remer did as instructed by Stauffenberg.

But Goebbels persuaded Remer to talk to Hitler's headquarters where he promised to put Hitler on and prove he was alive. Goebbels got through and Hitler came on the line. Hitler ordered Remer to obey Goebbels's instructions, to release anyone who had been arrested, and to remain in disciplined obedience to the government. Remer changed sides back to the Nazis immediately. He was subsequently rewarded and made a major general.

Kleist said Rommel was a simple, nonpolitical soldier. Early in the summer of 1944 he realized peace with the West must be made. On July 11, 1944, Lieutenant Colonel Caesar von Hofacker, an important figure at Rommel's headquarters, gave Kleist the impression that Rommel would back the plotters.

Kleist personally thought it was already too late to take any successful action. The plot no longer stood a chance of succeeding because the Allies would certainly not change their announced policy of unconditional surrender. But Kleist nevertheless thought it was still worth attempting the assassination for three reasons: (1) it was essential to Germany's honor for Germans to take some kind of action against the Nazis (2) by attempting the conspiracy, even if it didn't succeed, the war would be shortened and hundreds of thousands of lives saved (3) the plotters hoped that somehow they could arrange a cease-fire with the West and stave off Soviet occupation. Kleist said the first two points would have worked had Hitler been killed. That would have been something. He never thought there was any chance of the third point being accepted by the West.

Ewald's father, a distinguished Junker and fervent anti-Nazi, visited England twice. The second visit was a highly secret affair in 1940, after the fall of France. The elder Kleist went through Sweden and from there on to England. He wished to persuade those in power in London to take action so the German generals would be convinced of the necessity to rid themselves of Hitler.

Ewald's father did not get far. On his first private visit he never saw Churchill, who was not even prime minister yet, and ran into great difficulty with Robert Vansittart, of the foreign office, who had an important anti-German influence on the government of Chamberlain. Duff Cooper was also very anti-German. This was not just a question of being anti-Nazi but anti-German. Kleist added: "No man who makes foreign policy based on hate is any good."

The younger Kleist joined the conspiracy in 1941. He was not yet even an officer, just a private soldier in his regiment, formerly the First Guards Regiment, assigned to protect the German emperor. After the kaiser fled and World War I ended, the First Guards Regiment became the Ninth Infantry Regiment. However, it remained the most snobbish regiment in the German army and the aristocracy continued to provide practically all its officers. It was an excellent fighting group and strongly anti-Nazi.

Kleist became a second lieutenant in the Ninth in 1942. He found it filled with anti-Nazis. Five of its officers were executed for participation in the plot and ten or eleven of them actually also conspired. The initial move that Kleist actively took on behalf of the conspiracy was to act as a courier to arrange meetings. He first met Stauffenberg in January 1944. He had been allowed to go home on leave after being released from a hospital where he was treated for wounds received on the Russian front. Soon he received a telegram ordering him back to the regiment, then stationed at Potsdam. When he reported, the adjutant told him he could go home to the flat he shared with a fellow officer, young Count Werner von der Schulenberg who was in the plot and a good friend of Stauffenberg.

Rather to Kleist's horror, Schulenberg asked him to take a bomb and kill Hitler. Kleist and Schulenberg then went to see Stauffenberg to discuss the assassination. As Kleist tells it: "The plan was that I should be introduced to Hitler as an officer who had tried out various new uniforms on the front. Hitler was at that time very interested in uniforms. I was supposed to give him a report on their effectiveness and during our conversation, I was to kill him. This was to be in mid-February 1944. I would fly from Berlin to Rastenburg. But the day before my scheduled departure, the uniforms I was to bring were burned up in an RAF air raid. Therefore the project was put off."

This method of approaching Hitler had first been discussed with another officer, Axel Baron von dem Bussche. But Bussche was very badly wounded and disfigured in North Africa so it was impossible to use him.

By the time another specific attempt was planned by Stauffenberg, it was July and Hitler was no longer interested in uniforms. Some other method had to be found. The only conspirator with a logical reason to approach Hitler and take part in a conference at his general headquarters was Stauffenberg himself as chief of staff of the Home Army.

By the time of the July 20, 1944 action, Kleist had fully recovered from his wounds. Unfortunately, the plot was badly organized. There was so much confusion when the moment of crisis came that a great deal of action on an ad hoc basis was required. The plotters wanted to limit their conspiracy only to people they were positive they could trust.

Kleist himself was caught on July 20. He looked out of the window and saw a friend, a captain, rushing through the *Tiergarten*. Already there had been a great deal of confusion in Fromm's headquarters so Kleist chased after the captain to ask what was going on. The captain told him the plot was finished.

He was on his way out of Berlin and wanted to escape fast. Kleist told him he would shoot him unless he came back and helped. Then Olbricht asked Kleist if he would round up whatever police and soldiers he could because there simply were not enough armed persons available to the conspiracy. It proved impossible to get very many people.

Kleist had already prepared himself for possible failure by swiping a couple of blank movement orders of the highest grade — insuring that the man to whom they were made out could go anywhere speedily. He had not only taken the blanks but had affixed the proper rubber stamps. He had himself assigned to a battalion stationed on the Norwegian-Swedish border. That document was in his pocket on July 20.

But, he made the mistake of first going back to headquarters before taking off. He was arrested and taken to Stauffenberg's office where he was received by Otto Skorzeny, the famous SS officer who had rescued Mussolini from captivity after the duce's fall from power. Ewald was taken to the Gestapo prison on Prinz Albrecht Strasse and eventually on to Ravensbrück concentration camp. Kleist says he was probably one of the five hundred best-informed persons in Germany and yet he had never even heard of the existence of Ravensbrück. It was extraordinary the way these horrible camps were kept secret.

After about ten days at Ravensbrück he was returned to the Gestapo jail. Then he was moved to Tegel prison where military personnel expelled from the Wehrmacht were incarcerated. A lengthy interrogation began. He was summoned by the prison commander and when the guards left him outside, his face against a wall, to inform the commander that Kleist was ready, to his astonishment his father was brought into the same hall outside the commander's office and stood up next to him. They couldn't talk under the circumstances but at least he could see his father was alive. The elder Kleist was then fifty-four.

That was the next to last time Ewald saw him.

After the first interrogation he was returned to his cell. In fact, altogether he underwent thirty-two interrogations, none lasting less than three hours. He was scheduled to be tried in November 1944 before a people's court, but this did not happen. On December 6, 1944, the cell door opened and a guard came in and said: "You must prepare yourself to go."

"Where to?" Kleist asked.

"To the people's court," was the answer.

Kleist figured everything was up. He would obviously be convicted and executed immediately. To his astonishment, the guard who had summoned him said goodbye to him as he came to the end of the hall to be turned over to another guard. He had tears in his eyes and embraced Ewald. Then he said, without any change of expression: "I know you have a small piece of ham in your cell. You won't be needing it anymore. I'm sure you won't mind if I take it." He added: "Don't worry my boy. It isn't very painful. They just put a rope around your neck and it's all over in a second."

But instead of going to a people's court, Kleist was taken to Gestapo headquarters and the office of a high SS leader. The SS officer instructed the guards to remove Ewald's handcuffs, asked him to sit down, offered him a cigarette and told him that he was a free man. He was ordered to report to the office of the Gestapo in charge of liaison with the Wehrmacht.

Ewald reported to his new commanding major and was told he had been expelled from the Wehrmacht on December 14, 1944. That didn't break Kleist's heart. He returned to his flat and took a hot bath. While soaking in the water he reflected on the situation. He simply couldn't understand what was going on. Subsequently he talked to a Gestapo official, one of his many interrogators, a man who had been very nice to him. The Gestapo interrogator warned he was still under surveillance and told him the smartest thing he could do would be to go to the front. "But I have been expelled from the Wehrmacht," said Kleist.

"Never mind," said the Gestapo man. "Go anyway."

He then visited a friend who was a colonel in intelligence, a man who had refused as a matter of principle to participate in the plot because he did not think it was an honorable thing in time of war. This colonel, although he had declined to play any conspiratorial role, gave him a movement order to his own headquarters in Italy, near Rovereto. He also provided Kleist with movement orders to Ferrara and Genoa. In this way Ewald could move around continually in northern Italy and keep out of the way of the Gestapo. He recalls the colonel with gratitude, remarking that it was peculiar to have a man who had refused to get involved himself risk his life to give him these orders, knowing Ewald had been in the July 20 plot.

The last time Ewald saw his father was in prison. His father was tried in March 1945 and executed on April 16. He was a well-known anti-Nazi who, in 1929, in the first book he ever published, had warned against the growing Hitler movement and the possibility that it might take power. A large Pomeranian landed estate owner, he was head of the Conservative party.

It was a very strange thing for Ewald to be able to see him not too many months before his death. The prison where Ewald was at that time confined was staffed by the SS. One noncommissioned officer of the SS was very friendly to Ewald. He used to come by his cell at night, open the door and give him bread and sausage to eat. This was peculiar because the man also — although he was very kind to Ewald — was a complete son of a bitch. He used to tell him about the horrible things the SS had done in Poland to the poor Polish people; how they tortured and slaughtered them.

Yet, he said to Ewald one night, after producing food for him, that he was puzzled by the fact that another man with exactly the same name was in the same prison, another man named Ewald von Kleist. "But of course that's my father," Ewald said. So the SS man came by one night and illegally took him to his father's cell, tactfully leaving the two together. They were unable to talk about important things because they were afraid the cell might be bugged. But they did exchange some information. Ewald asked if his father had been tortured. His father said no. They had slapped him once and he had told the slapper: "If you ever do that again I'll never say another word." Afraid that they might lose a potentially valuable witness, they never touched him again.

Summing up the plot, Ewald said: "The main reason for the failure was the lack of realization that you cannot overthrow a dictatorship without the use of power, violence, and force. It was necessary to shoot people in order to succeed. But the conspirators didn't want to shed blood. This put them in an impossible position."

Not even General Ludwig Beck, who was to have been proclaimed head of the new German government after Hitler's death, could see that it was necessary to use violence, nor could Stauffenberg and Schulenberg. Ewald continued: "It's very difficult to communicate under a dictatorship. You must first know that a man is reliable. And there were just a very few available people who were thoroughly reliable. Even fewer of these were in positions of authority where they could take effective action.

"There was a small resistance front in Germany which included several different groups — that of Karl Goerdeler, former mayor of Leipzig; the Kreisau Circle; and the Stauffenberg group. But they were not coordinated. They vaguely knew about each other but that was all. Even in the Stauffenberg group, no member of the conspiracy was told more than he absolutely needed to know. This of course helped security but on the other hand made for a great deal of misunderstanding."

Ewald says Stauffenberg and Schulenberg were both very important to the plot. Schulenberg's role was enormous. He explained to Stauffenberg and a few other high conspirators that Hitler simply had to be killed. Stauffenberg himself, a very brave man who had been desperately wounded, was quite ready to blow himself up with Hitler when it was finally decided that he should take the bomb to headquarters. But Beck ordered him not to do this. He said it was essential that Stauffenberg should stay alive after Hitler's death because all the strings of the conspiracy came together in his mind alone. He was absolutely irreplaceable. It was Stauffenberg and also General von Gersdorff, Count von Schwerin, who planned the actual July 20 operation. But many different decisions affecting the plot were made by different groups of conspirators. These were not coordinated and left a muddle.

An astonishing tale this, attended by Christopher; and insufficiently understood by him — or indeed, the world. I suspect the little beagle was reflecting: "What a nice man. But those people he was talking about, those Nazis. They shouldn't do such things to each other, to humans. Dogs would never do such things to each other. Or to anyone. I am glad the gentleman tried to kill Mr. Hitler. I would have bitten him to death."

 XII Returned to Athens en route to Jugoslavia and Austria. Costa Caramanlis invited me for dinner at the luxurious new Hotel Astir Palace on the sea at Vouliagmeni, about twenty miles from Athens. The sensation of the evening wasn't the prime minister but the guests of honor, Dr. Christiaan Barnard, South African heart-transplant surgeon, and his wife. She, born in Germany but reared in South Africa, is the most beautiful woman I've ever seen; and very nice to boot.

He's here helping plan and launch a large hotel and sanitorium complex on the island of Cos where Hippocrates was born. An engineer-promoter dreamed up the scheme and I was shown plans and mock-ups. It's most impressive and should leap to the forefront of European spas because of its beautiful setting and promised expert medical staff for those who want checkups, etc., in addition to relaxed pleasure.

Christopher and I arrived at the grandiose new Macedonian resort of Porto Carras on the last day of June as guests of Director General Costa Stavropoulos, a man close to seventy and the son of a general who had been a great hero in the Greek wars against the Bulgarians and the Turks that preceded World War I.

The general had been posted in one city in Macedonia after another and his family went along. The present Stavropoulos got to know the province very well and developed a huge love for it. His sister married John Carras, a wealthy Greek shipowner. Thanks largely to the family connection, they conceived the idea of a vast development scheme to improve the still rather obscure area. They formed a company with the idea of attracting a large number of tourists and it has three divisions. One runs an enormous hotel complex; another handles agriculture and wine production; a third handles exports and imports. The shipping side is an unconnected branch.

The Porto Carras company managed to raise money partly through private investment and partly through government loans, to buy eighteen thousand *stremata* (about forty-five hundred acres) of magnificent land along the sea from some of the monasteries of Mount Athos, which is a few miles away on the three-pronged peninsula of Khalkidhikí. To accomplish this, a special law was passed. Then the company hired Walter Gropius, the famous German architect who died an American citizen. This enterprise is the last project Gropius undertook.

It is a beautiful region of thick pine forests, olive orchards, vineyards, and grain fields. The hotel complex is just opening and I am the first guest in one of the two hotels that will eventually operate.

The hotels look like huge fortresses. They are about a quarter of a mile apart facing each other along a beach, each eight stories high and designed to hold a thousand guests. Only one opens this year. There is an eighteen-hole golf course beside it.

Nikolaos Martis, minister of northern Greece, arranged for me (minus Christopher) to take off in Stavropoulos's car to Athos early in the morning and to have the driver deliver my luggage to my car in a Salonika garage. The following afternoon, Martis's car would pick me up at the border of the holy mountain.

We were driven to Ouranopoulos, last village of Greece proper before one crosses the frontier to Athos: two and a half hours across a winding mountainous route. We drove through thick forests of huge strange trees with large, yellow-fingered tropical blossoms. We whizzed past a place once known as Stagira, marking the site where Aristotle was born.

We came out at the westernmost of the three prongs of Khalkidhikí, the peninsula east of Salonika, which was crossed by Xerxes' army when he invaded Greece in the fifth century B.C. In order to keep his troops near their supply ships, he drove two canals across the narrow points of the easternmost and the westernmost fingers. After waiting for a half hour at Ouranopoulos, a small resort village, a little ferryboat took me aboard and we set off for Mount Athos, leaving a forlorn Christopher behind with the driver. I sat on the forward deck with a priest reading his holy psalter — a pale-faced, black-bearded, black-eyed, black-hatted, black-gowned man.

First we chugged by green rocks over a calm blue-green sea. There was a gentle southerly breeze. Soon a great tree-covered block of mountains rose on our left as we headed southward. It was not high but it was protected by a sheer cliff. Occasionally one could spot rare monasteries or stone houses hidden among the trees or near the shore. The heights rose eventually up to a great peak which is snow-covered in winter and is over six thousand feet high. We stopped at the pier of one monastery after another, each time to pick up a single traveling monk heading to another holy institution. Happy schools of dolphins jumped and frisked in the sea about a hundred yards to the starboard side.

Finally, we reached tiny Daphni, the biggest port on Mount Athos but still only a hamlet. There I was met by the governor's secretary, Dimitrios Bambakas, a fat, short, bearded, nonclerical layman who is nevertheless unusually religious. He crossed himself more than any priest I've ever seen. Before each meal he crossed himself three times and then twice afterward. When we traveled by road he crossed himself at every curve and almost every tree we passed. He told me I must cross myself in the monastery when meals were served and during church services. I tried this once and then stopped. It seemed silly to follow his ideas of politeness when all the monks knew that I was not Orthodox. Bambakas explained to me that the governor, Dimitrios Tsamis, was away but would return the next day in his own little speedboat.

We climbed into a Land Rover driven by a man on Bambakas's staff. There are few nonclericals on the island — a handful of government officials, their servants, representatives of the telegraph and telephone company, some gendarmes, and occasional workers who come out to special jobs either for the government or for the monks.

The road up to the capital, Karyes, is exceptionally bad. It penetrates a low forest and is lined by thick blackberry bushes. There are numerous wildflowers all over the peninsula. As we bumped along, covered with dust, Dimitri talked. He said the mountain which we could easily see to our right as we headed toward Karyes is 2,033 meters high. Karyes is six hundred meters high. Its population is only a hundred and fifty. This includes one hundred monks and fifty functionaries, police, telephone people, post office and temporary workers.

Bambakas chatted in French, which he speaks fluently, having studied theology in Paris for four years. He invited me to lunch shortly after we arrived. The driver and I were each served string beans cooked in oil and two Greek hamburgers *(keftedes)*. Dimitri only ate the beans. There was also bread and water from the private spring of the governor's house-office where all of them live. Bambakas explained that he ate no meat because it was a saint's day and semifast.

He said some of the monks are well-educated. There is one American, some Germans and British, but all these are of Slav origin. The total religious population is about fourteen hundred monks scattered among twenty monasteries and smaller establishments and cells. He said that a few of the wealthier monasteries have limited electricity provided by themselves. The others use kerosene lamps. The cooking everywhere is done either with wood fires or bottles of gas. There are no television sets on the island but radios are permitted. Generally these are used to listen only to news programs. The government office has a telephone and so do some monasteries.

Dimitri suggested we visit Moni Stavronikita, a sixteenth-century monastery of the cenobetic rite.

While he prepared himself for the trip, I read swiftly through a heavy but excellent book written in French by a Greek theological student. It says there were five or six towns on Mount Athos in antiquity. All were abandoned in the early centuries after Christ, long before the monks came. In the ninth and tenth centuries, Slav shepherds descended the peninsula. They were followed by Vlachs in the twelfth century. The first mention of any monks found in documents is in the ninth century. The tradition of Mount Athos claims the emperor Constantine the Great founded the first convents here in the fourth century but that they were destroyed by the emperor Julian the Apostate.

The land of the peninsula is divided up among the twenty monasteries, although not on an equal basis. Some are very wealthy and some very poor. In addition to monasteries, there are monastic villages of separate houses called *skaete,* comprising groups of buildings around a central church. There are twelve *skaete* at Mount Athos. Each belongs to a monastery; sometimes two or three to a single monastery. *Skaete* monks work as painters, wood carvers, or at other creative labor in order to earn their living.

Then there are what are called cells. There are still from six to seven hundred of these, but they are steadily declining in number. They are mostly agricultural communities of three or four monks each who till the soil and work as foresters.

There is also another type of holy dwelling called *isikhastiria* (hesychasts): small houses with several members of each community. They make icons and are closely bound by a very strict regimen of prayers; the most rigorous of all the theological divisions on the peninsula.

There are *kathismata* as well: houses which are near the monasteries and dependent on them. The *igumen*, or abbot, of each monastery governs their activity. The *kathismata* members pray almost as much as the *isikhastiria*. Finally, among subordinate communities, there are hermits who generally live alone in caves. They spend their entire time in prayer and contemplation and, occasionally, cultivating or soliciting food.

The bulk of the population is in the twenty big monasteries. These are divided into two types according to their form of administration. There are the cenobetic, where all monks live and take their meals together under the administration of an *igumen*, and the *ithiorythma*, which have no *igumen* but are each run by a small directing committee of about four. Monks of this sort pray together but do not eat together. The monastery pays each monk enough to provide for his needs. This system, begun during the Turkish occupation, is less stern and rigid than the cenobetic rite.

Dimitri finally prepared himself, changing his shoes, shirt, and trousers, packing a little bag and putting on a hat. He took with him a long stave of cherry wood which, he explained, was used to kill vipers. Although we walked a good deal, I didn't see any sign of a snake.

We drove in the Land Rover down to the eastern shore of the peninsula by a large old tower which was once used as a fortification against pirate raiders. There are many such towers, well fortified. They were manned by monks assisted by occasional armed laymen from among the workers who came to do special jobs.

Then we struck off along the shore on a rough path, finally
following a mule, much tormented by huge flies, who was wandering along without a saddle. He led us along a narrow trail
through underbrush to the great monastery. The only animals of
burden allowed on the island are mules and male donkeys.

We were very hot and sweaty when we reached the gate of the
monastery, set on a high cliff above the sea, and were greeted by
a tall old monk. He seated us in a trellised grape arbor, cool and
fresh, and brought us each a glass of cold water, a small glass of
tsipuro, and a sweet — what we call Turkish delight. Father
Theodosius, the monk who acted so hospitably, stood while we
relaxed and drank, regarding us gravely. After that he led Bambakas and myself up to our clean, bare rooms on the top floor of
the monastery, overlooking the shadow of the distant island of
Thassos.

According to Dimitri, the present monastery was built in the
sixteenth century. It is made of stone and has a central fortified
tower rising high above the other buildings and topped with
crenellations. The roofs of the main buildings are of slate. In the
center of the courtyard, squeezed up against the walls so that it
never receives any air and is breathlessly hot, is the rose-colored
central church.

Bambakas told me the *igumen* of Stavronikita is named Vassilios. He was born in Crete and studied for a while in France.
He speaks French and is very learned although only forty-three
years old. We sat in the trellised arbor and talked, then walked
up and down inspecting enormous tall cypress and chestnut
trees.

The call for vespers was sounded by a hammered iron ring and
wooden drum and we followed the monks into the lovely little
church every inch of which, including the walls and ceiling, was
adorned with sixteenth-century paintings or icons. We sat in tall
chairs in the apse. Only monks and Greek Orthodox visitors are
allowed to enter the inner sanctuary at the very end of the service. The floor is composed of white stone slabs.

As we filed in, to the counterpoint of the iron ring and wooden tom-tom — a long bar beaten with a mallet by a novice — I counted the number of actual monks in the congregation. There were twenty including the *igumen*, a six-foot, green-eyed man with a nose like a scimitar, a handsome face and bearing, well-tended beard and mustache. Later, when he took off his black hat outside, I discovered that he is almost bald. I imagine those black felt monks' hats — different from the ordinary priests' hats which are higher and less heavy — must be very bad for the hair; no air can circulate beneath them. All the monks wore black gowns and black hats covered with flowing black shawls which, together with the blackness of their mustaches and beards, seemed to hide their faces from the world.

The vesper services lasted a long time. There were continual mournful Byzantine chants. I got a creepy feeling as the monks bent in the semidarkness and touched the ground and crossed themselves, occasionally moving forward to kiss one icon after another. Finally, after the suffocatingly hot and lengthy service, Igumen Vassilios took me outside and we sat on a long wall and conversed in French, brushed by the evening breeze. Later I was told by a visiting French deacon from the Greek Orthodox community of Marseilles, that the *igumen* had studied both in Paris and in Lyon.

The *igumen* told me the monastery had existed in the eleventh century but was destroyed by pirates. The central tower actually was constructed in the tenth century. However, the monastery was rebuilt in the sixteenth century. Emperor John Tzimisces in the tenth century began the codified legal rule that no creature of the female sex could be tolerated on the holy peninsula. Of course there were never any women permitted in the monasteries or on the peninsula but there had not been a written law until Tzimisces. Even then, in the tenth century, the Grand Lavra monastery was allowed to keep a small herd of cows but these were never closer than twelve kilometers away from the monastery itself.

There have always been one or two exceptions but they are minor and rare. The code instituted by Tzimisces was made even more rigid during the next century by Emperor Constantine Monomachus. He sent a monk in his confidence to visit Mount Athos and to suggest certain basic laws. Together with the visiting monk from the emperor, they drew up a code which was brought back to Constantinople where Constantine signed it.

The *igumen* said there are no cows left on the peninsula but there are a few hens. In the old days, sometimes when a monk fell ill, he required milk. But nowadays it can be imported, just like cheese, from normal nontheological Greece. (I wonder why they can't do the same thing with eggs rather than having hens of their own.)

The *igumen* explained that the peninsula is of course part of Greece but it has a separate status all its own. The governor is responsible to the Ministry of Foreign Affairs whereas all other Greek districts are run by prefects responsible to the Ministry of the Interior.

A foreign monk who wishes to become a member of the community on Mount Athos must first have the permission of his church and then the patriarchate of Constantinople. If the patriarch's office passes him, he is allowed to come on a temporary basis to the holy mountain until they see how well he fits into the community. The minute he arrives at Mount Athos he becomes a Greek citizen and his passport is handed to the Ministry of Foreign Affairs.

A novice is allowed in a monastery between one and three years. If he fits in with the others and if he still likes the life there, he is then allowed to become a full monk. After that point he cannot resign; he is in the community for life.

Stavronikita has twenty monks and five novices at this moment. Vassilios says there is no problem finding monks; there are always sufficient applications. (I'm not sure this is true because certainly Stavronikita, for example, needs a great many more than it has to accomplish its farming work. And I am told this is true of other monasteries.)

The *igumen* said each monk is assigned work according to his capacity. He added: "We work hard. We have no problem of an economic sort. We do our own artistic restorations together with somebody sent from the Ministry of Culture in Athens. Several members of the community had other professions in their previous lives. Thus we have a dentist here who is a monk. Each monastery has its own pharmacy and one monk is trained as a pharmacist." According to Vassilios, if any monk is asked what his country is, he only replies: "My country is Mount Athos."

Our conversation was interrupted once more by prayers, this time the evening service. It was virtually dark except for two small tapers flickering in the apse. The service went on and on as the monks and the *igumen* and others who read the service kept repeating "Lord have mercy, Lord have mercy; *Kyrie Eleison, Kyrie Eleison.*" I found the rite almost intolerably long, hot and stuffy in the dark. The apse smelled strongly of garlic and sweat.

When it concluded, we went upstairs for dinner. We sat silently at long tables and the *igumen* sat alone at a small table at the far end. We were served cold stringbeans cooked in oil, olives, one fig, and bread. There was cold water. The food was on a tin plate. A gloomy young monk read from the life of the saint whose anniversary was being commemorated by the semifast, standing at a lectern, while all the rest of us ate silently.

Afterward, although it was dark, I was allowed to inspect the church with a torch. It is really lovely. There were some splendid paintings by a Cretan monk named Theophanes, predecessor of El Greco and Poulakis, the more famous seventeenth-century Cretan painters. Following this, we went up to our rooms. I lit my kerosene lamp and for a while, I read although it was hard going because the lamp was very weak. I read that Emperor John Tzimisces signed his act banning any creature of the female sex in 972. Emperor Constantine Monomachus signed his revision in the year 1045. Each emperor published the law governing Mount Athos in what was called in those days a chrysobull, listing the regulations. Women, men without beards, eunuchs, and young boys were banned or expelled. No flocks of sheep or goats were permitted; nor were any cattle except the cows Lavra was allowed under the first chrysobull.

When I could read no more because my eyes were watering, I blew out the light and lay in the humid hot night while mosquitoes buzzed all around me. Outside I could hear swallows dashing among the leaves. It seemed to be the season when they had just laid their eggs and, as I stood in the courtyard entrance to the church, I had noticed that swallows came and tried to frighten me away because I might disturb the hatching process in the nests attached to the walls high above. The monks apparently are not worried about the sex life of wild birds.

Around four o'clock in the morning, prayers were called once again, held in a little chapel apart from the monastery — two hundred yards away, above the sea. Some monks were apparently excused from these early prayers and were already working in the fields before dawn. It must be hard to do heavy farming in this heat while wearing black hats and long black robes.

We then went to breakfast, which still honored the fast: tea, halva (a sweet made of sesame seed and sugar), olives. The sesame is supposed to be very nourishing. I also noticed on each table a tin plate with large cloves of garlic in it. This explained the odor in the church. After breakfast we climbed to our rooms and assembled our few belongings.

The deacon from Marseilles, a very friendly fellow, told me most monks are laic, not priests. The *igumen* is a priest. We walked together back to the Land Rover which was waiting for us and drove to Karyes. There, Dimitri took me to visit the principal members of the governing organization which administers the quasi-autonomous republic under the benevolent eye of the governor. There is first of all an assembly called the Holy Community which comprises twenty people, one delegate from each monastery. It takes decisions by a majority vote. Its origin dates back to the tenth century. Then there is a small group of four, delegated by the twenty, which has executive power. The four are also members of the larger Holy Community.

There are five groups of monasteries arbitrarily linked together in blocs of four to make the entire community of twenty. The five ranked first in each group of four monasteries name a head of the Holy Community. He is called the protos and is chief of state, as it were, but he has no right to vote in decisions.

The Holy Council, or parliament, can request things like roads or government help from the state and these are approved by the four-man executive committee, then authorized by the protos who forwards suggestions to the governor, representing the Greek Foreign Ministry. The governor communicates them to Athens for action.

The protos remains in office one year. At present, he is a monk from Dionysiou Monastery. He is a kind of a protocol chief of state. His office is in the same building as the Holy Council and the four-man executive.

Dimitri and I walked to this building through the little hamlet of Karyes. There are a few small shops, all owned by the monasteries, some tended by monks or novices, some by nonclerics such as visiting workmen.

Opposite the main building of the monks' administration is the tenth-century church of Protathon, named for the protos. Before visiting the church, Dimitri took me up to the office of Protos Theoclitos, a very friendly man, about five foot ten with graying beard, heavy spectacles, and smiling countenance. He spoke only Greek, which Bambakas interpreted. The protos gave me an honorary residence permit for Mount Athos. I noticed his office walls were decorated with pictures of the patriarchs of the Serbian church, the Bulgarian church, and other Orthodox communities; but not the Russian church. He told us that the Russian patriarch never sent him his photograph.

The protos explained the reason behind the rule forbidding female animals: "Mount Athos lives without any sexual life. Therefore to prevent anyone from seeing sexual life, female animals are banned." The Greek state had taken legal measures to ban all women who sought to enter the territory. They were fined and sent to prison from between three months to one year. However, during certain wars, including the Independence War in 1821 and the civil war that followed World War II, women fleeing for their lives were allowed to land in boats and stay on Mount Athos as a temporary refuge.

After saying goodbye to the protos, we went to the church of Protathon. Although it is from the tenth century, the frescoes are from the fourteenth century. I noted hanging inside the church the double-headed Byzantine eagle against a white background which is the patriarch's flag, and also the royal Greek flag of blue and white with a large golden crown in the middle. There was no flag of the present republic.

We then took the Land Rover down to Daphni to meet the governor, whose boat was due. From Daphni I was to go back to Ouranopoulos. We sat at a little tavern and drank retsina until Governor Tsamis showed up in his little boat: a friendly youthful man, far more modern in appearance and manner than Bambakas. He spoke excellent English and told me he was a professor of theology at Salonika University, although in no sense a priest.

He said the peninsula's principal exports, sent out by caiques, are wood and hazelnuts. When Caramanlis was here in 1976, he called Mount Athos "the oldest democracy in the world." Governor Tsamis thinks this is probably right although I thought Iceland might actually have an older parliament.

There are some non-Greek-speaking monasteries where only Russian or Serbian or Bulgarian or Rumanian are spoken and where prayers are said in Old Slavonic instead of Greek.

One of the governor's jobs is to act as a kind of private agent on behalf of the Greek government to ensure that no undesirables are admitted from abroad as monks. For example, some Soviet espionage agents tried to infiltrate the holy mountain but were prevented. Tsamis travels around interviewing authorities in countries from which people apply. He is also involved in the expulsion of undesirables reported to him by the *igumen* of each monastery when this occurs. The moment a man is expelled as a monk his old passport is returned to him and his Greek passport is taken away.

Some monasteries are really quite rich. They have money invested outside of Mount Athos in industry or real estate. The role of the government is only to supervise and authorize the selling of property like Porto Carras. It has nothing to do with the handling of the income of each monastery. Some, like Stavronikita, are very poor. But although the government would like rich institutions to share with their poorer fellows, they don't. The poor must make do for themselves. They are helped out, however, by government subsidies.

Strangely enough, Tsamis added, poor monasteries have much more success in recruiting new monks than rich ones. They attract intelligent, young, new recruits who are bitter toward outside life.

The governor told me that certain monasteries have an immensely shrunken number of monks because of their "bad habits" — implying homosexuality. He said: "They get no new recruits." Also, they like to discourage people from applying because they are intent on "avoiding exposure."

But on the whole, he said, there is not much of a problem in keeping up the monastic population. Many middle-class youths come to Mount Athos to escape from the outer world. They already know discotheques, cars, and television. They want serenity. They don't approach Mount Athos via the normal Greek church establishment but through agents of the different monasteries sent to various cities of Greece.

The governor and Bambakas came down to the pier with me. I was interested to see that my large briefcase was opened. There is a customs inspection of all baggage departing from Mount Athos to be sure no relics or icons are being smuggled out. After the inspection I said goodbye. Tsamis told me that he would happily invite my daughter to take an offshore cruise on his motorboat so she could see the monasteries from the sea. He also told me that next time I could bring Christopher all the way since he is a male.

We waved farewell as the boat set off and soon were in Ouranopoulos. There, Martis's large Mercedes car was waiting, with Christopher gazing eagerly toward the landing. He raised his tail and squealed with pleasure as I stepped ashore.

XIII   Traveled to Jugoslavia for some trout-fishing with a muted Christopher. I mistrusted the little beagle's fate among the wild sheep dogs, yet he tactfully survived. In Belgrade, before taking off, we again stayed with Ambassador Larry Eagleburger. He used to be one of Henry Kissinger's top men in the state department, and he told me an interesting thing. I had mentioned that Kissinger, while still national security advisor, told me he could not possibly get involved in Middle Eastern affairs and was glad to leave them in the hands of Secretary of State Bill Rogers because Henry was a Jew and it was impossible for him to intervene. I had never believed this and thought Kissinger was always planning to involve himself.

Larry said the story was quite true. However, Henry did once say to Dean Acheson he felt that he should stay out of Middle Eastern affairs because he was a Jew. In that case, Dean told him, "You can never hope to be secretary of state. You should give up such complexes."

Took a four-day fishing holiday with Christopher and Djilas, now regarded as "public enemy number one" by the Tito regime. Yet in his day, Djilas was number two to Tito alone in the Communist hierarchy. He has had a strange and unhappy life. From 1933 to 1936 he was in prison in Belgrade under the royal regime as an accused Communist. He was tortured but refused to give any evidence. Then from 1956 to 1961 he was in jail again as a renegade Communist. This resulted from an interview he gave to a foreign correspondent on the Hungarian uprising in 1956.

He had already written articles in *Borba,* the party newspaper, in which he criticized corruption and power-grabbing by a "new class" of bureaucrats as a result of the revolution. Then his book *The New Class* was published abroad in 1957 while he was in prison. As a consequence, his original sentence was increased. However, in 1961 he was conditionally released on parole. He was considered to have violated this by publishing another book, called *Conversations with Stalin.* Before the book was published he had sent me the manuscript and asked me to write a couple of columns on it, which I did.

All in all he has spent twelve years in prison. Considering that he is sixty-eight now, that is not a bad record. Add to that four years as a partisan leader fighting the Axis and one can see that he has had a turbulent life.

In 1954, he was expelled from his governmental position, from his membership in the political bureau of the Communist party, from his membership in the central committee, and from his membership in the Jugoslav Fishermen's Association. This shows how screwy things can get.

This was the first fishing expedition he had been on since 1954 — a twenty-five year lapse which in some ways was as hard a punishment as any other. Furthermore, with the exception of the year 1968, when he was allowed to go abroad briefly, he has not been permitted to leave the country.

Our trip was to the northeastern corner of Serbia called the Homoljske. This is a lovely, soft, hilly area replete with woods and many rivers, and Christopher explored thoroughly. The Homoljske has a mysterious history. In one corner, near the Bulgarian border, when I first came to Jugoslavia forty-odd years ago, there was a famous dance every spring in which all the women gradually fainted, one by one, in a trance. As they lay unconscious, the men danced around them. Then, chewing garlic, they went to a neighboring stream, filled their mouths with water and spat through crossed knives upon the women, who came to immediately. Even baby girls and little children fell under the trance. It is something psychiatrists have not yet explained.

Also, the Homoljske was known for its *hajduks*. These were robber chieftains or brigands like Robin Hood. They began in the Middle Ages under the Turkish occupation. They tried to rob the rich and often gave to the poor. As a consequence, people protected them and hid them from the authorities.

We ate dinner in a *privat*, or privately owned restaurant, called the Homoljac, meaning "the man from Homoljske." There we were generally in the company of fishermen, including a most pleasant ex-policeman and his son. The policeman, aged fifty-eight, was retired and looked like a successful central European banker, well dressed and always with a good briar pipe. Another was a fellow named Brača Miličević.

He told us an amusing story of the motel where we sometimes ate lunch (dinner was impossible because of the incredibly noisy electronic music) and where he and his wife stayed. It is situated on the upper pool of the Mlava River, a forbidden fishing zone for about three hundred yards, and filled with large fish. Once, Brača hung a line out from his window, baited with meat, and caught a large trout illegally. He said: "Everyone was breaking the law and I couldn't catch anything. That is I couldn't catch anything elsewhere. So I started breaking the law myself."

The area contains high fields of corn in meadows all around the Mlava which, lined by thick bushes and willows, flows gently through a broad valley bordered by the Homoljske hills of eastern Serbia. Peasant women in shawls and heavy skirts were tossing hay with primitive wooden pitchforks. Along the river, which I fished for twelve kilometers, there were a couple of rickety wicker bridges, one comprising only a single bent, thin log with a fragile handrail of a single branch.

We stayed at the dreary little village of Zagubica in a fourth-class autobus hotel, an unkempt place with no restaurant. But they were very pleasant to us. Everybody was nice, including the chief of police, another gendarme, and the waiter, who personally fed Christopher. The countryside and the human atmosphere were absolutely tranquil.

At first, Milovan was a bit nervous — he hadn't fished for so long, and had only just been readmitted to the Fisherman's Association. He was also somewhat worried about his reception in the village, being convinced that the police at Belgrade had tapped his telephone and then called ahead tipping people off. He was very proud of his new rod.

Like Djilas, all the other anglers were spinner men. I caught three one-kilo trout as well as several others which I released. Christopher swam daintily. The river is extremely difficult because it is completely overhung with trees; also, it is fished so much by the local spinner men that the trout are very spooky. But there are plenty if one is careful. You have to get into the water to have any chance of casting a fly. I stood from six to eight hours a day in the stream — without boots. The only noise, apart from the gurgling of the water, was the sound of the birds.

I was impressed by the utter peace. There were ramshackle fences that had to be crossed to make one's way up or down. Herd girls tended their flocks, quietly spinning wool by hand. At one point, I saw two turkeys and eight ducks lethargically lying in the shade beside the silently gliding river. The Mlava is curious. Its source is at Zagubica where it flows right out of the side of a mountain. There isn't a single trickle; the river just starts suddenly like a great pool. And the left-hand fork, when you go downstream, abruptly disappears entirely into the ground again. First there is water, then there is field.

Milovan told me about his last fishing trip. It took place in 1954 after his overthrow from power. He was with a group of five anglers who rode a raft together down the Drina River, starting from Foča. For ten days the current bore them down a canyon. At night they slept onshore in tents. They used all means of fishing, including spinners and live fish. They tied gang hooks around the live fish and sometimes attached them by heavy line to the raft. They also cast and trolled.

The river was about fifty-five meters wide and very deep. It was filled with whirlpools and bright blue in color. They covered about two hundred kilometers and stopped at Perušic, on the Serbian-Bosnian border. Milovan said he had very good luck. At the inflow of one of the tributaries of the Drina he caught seven trout. He also caught one seven-kilo landlocked salmon, called a *huch,* at Mladenovac.

The raft had a rudder at the stern. They used poles to get it away from obstacles. At waterfalls and heavy rapids, everybody had to get off and remove everything stored aboard. Then they would let the raft drift down until it came to calm water again. It broke often and they would catch it, push it into a pool and repair it. They carried all the necessary tools, including saws, hammers, nails, and wires to tie logs together. Each person had bags of belongings, tents, sleeping bags.

There were a lot of snakes which were always cleared away by the party before they chose a place to sleep. In fishing for *huch,* they prepared live fish with hooks on them and cast them from the shore near the camp with heavy, stiff rods and a heavy, high-test line with nylon leader.

The last fish he had caught in all these twenty-five years was that 1954 *huch.* It was taken in the evening when it was quite dark. There was a pool two hundred meters long. He walked along the shore to the middle of it, and on the second cast the fish took the bait. It didn't fight hard. He didn't even have to use a gaff. A friend held his rod and he got below the fish in the water, moved up gently, finally getting beside it and lifting it with both hands and casting it on the shore. They ate it the same night, roasted over a wood fire.

This year, he at last went back to the fishing society's headquarters and asked if he could rejoin. Strangely enough, the same man who had been secretary when he was expelled was still there. He said to Milovan: "I gave you your first membership. Then there were some political problems." He was friendly but definitely nervous.

I asked Milovan what he thinks is the special appeal of fishing. He said: "When I was twelve, in 1923, I watched a famous fisherman angle. I watched him fish with worms and both natural and artificial insects. He had a light rod and he also used frogs and live fish. He was a poor man seeking food but he adored fishing. This was on the famous lake of Biogradsko Jezero.

"He fished regularly there and also in some of the rivers of the region. He was our neighbor in the village of Podbišće. He was a peasant with a little land near the river but it was bad, rocky land and he was so poor that one of his sons died of hunger during the Austrian occupation of World War I. I remember that although I was a little boy at the time I was shocked and horrified. He often said to me that if he didn't fish, his family would starve to death. He made his own hooks.

"As a result of this experience I made a rod of hazelnut wood. But the tip was of even harder wood. I made a line of braided white horsehair from a horse's tail. It was very difficult to find the properly long and properly white tail of a horse and pluck a few hairs until you had enough to braid them together. The leader I used was imported gut. I bought it and the hooks. I put worms and insects on the hooks. One of my favorites was a kind of green-banded locust.

"I became a passionate fisherman. We caught trout differently. We didn't play them slowly. We had no reel to let out line. We just had a little line and jerked the fish out of the water so it fell on the grass or in a tree. And we were very careful with our lines because it was so hard to find horses with long white tails.

"I think people like fishing because there is some eternal connection between man and fish, especially trout. I think maybe life started in a way between man and trout. Trout is the highest form of fish for man to associate with.

"Also trout tastes marvelous. It is hard to catch. It is intelligent and it fights well. There are many elements involved.

"In fishing, it is also important, most important, to have a chance to dream and to think. Trout always live in beautiful surroundings and clean cold water. I find this stimulating.

"I think if I didn't fish with such enthusiasm I would not have rebelled against the central committee. My thoughts became clarified as I fished. My individuality and integrity developed. Subconsciously I changed.

"Also as a writer there was a change in me. My mind cleared away unimportant thoughts. In this way I discovered and improved many of the motifs of my books. You are both active and inactive when you fish trout. Part of the mind concentrates on finding and attracting and catching the fish. But part of the mind is free to think of original thoughts untarnished by city life and modern complexities.

"Perhaps one feels as prehistoric man felt. I feel I am doing what pre-Slavic, Bronze Age, and Stone Age people did. You go beyond civilization — before it. Maybe even the fisherman goes beyond and before man himself."

Right after our return, I drove with Christopher all the way from Belgrade deep into Greece. As we were going past Mount Olympus, along the coastal road in Macedonia, I saw, to my astonishment, a great V-shaped flight of wild geese flapping heavily northward over the mountain.

Next day I zipped through Athens and on to Costa, the coastal village opposite Spetsais. My daughter and grandchildren had arrived on holiday and were overjoyed to see Christopher.

 Mordekhai Gazit and his pretty wife Rina came to lunch in Spetsais that August. He had been Israeli ambassador in Paris for the last four years and was returning to Jerusalem for a new assignment.

They said with joy: "At last, after four months, we don't have to have a security guard around us." Apparently Israeli intelligence warned them of a plot against him and the military attaché, even giving them the numbers of an automobile which drove into Germany carrying the would-be killers. Gazit advised the protocol department of the French Foreign Ministry which is charged with assigning security guards to protect ambassadors. But French protocol only looks after the safety of chiefs of mission. The military attaché had to make his own arrangements.

The Israelis, not trusting French efficiency, sent two of their security men to Paris with false documents listing them as special technicians on the embassy staff — without diplomatic protection. The poor Gazits have been tailed everywhere by these protectors.

There is no Greek ambassador in Israel, only a "diplomatic representative." Caramanlis has twice informed Israel that Greece would like to have full relations but the project has been put off so many years that it is now difficult to change.

Mordekhai, a youthful-looking man of fifty-eight with only a touch of gray at the temples, was gravely wounded and nearly killed in 1948 during the first Israeli-Arab war, which established Israel's independence. He led a reinforcing unit of ninety men into the old city of Jerusalem which was in the process of being taken over by Jordan's Arab Legion. In the end, the Arabs won. Gazit was shot twice by machine-gun bullets next to the heart. The bullets entered his lungs and exited through his back. He was left for dead. However, there were three doctors in the sector of battle: a Red Cross man, an Arab Legion physician, and an Israeli physician. Mordekhai said the Arab Legion man was by far the best. Thanks to him Mordekhai is alive today.

One September day, Christopher and I went with Adonis and Caroline Kyrou on their boat to Kilada, northwest of Kraní dhion, to visit the enormous Francthi Cave. Now it is situated about ninety or one hundred feet above the water and the entrance is largely blocked by fallen rock. But some fifteen thousand to twenty-five thousand years ago, the entrance was on a flat plateau extending over the portion of the Aegean Sea which runs in there now along the present Gulf of Nauplia. The withdrawal of the Ice Age brought water into the plain but some terrible volcanic explosion on the distant Italian island of Ischia filled the cave with ash. Then earth tremors knocked hundreds of boulders out of the ceiling, partially blocking the entrance and cutting the cave in two.

Two archaeologists and a visiting professor from the University of Pennsylvania came along with us and explained. It has been a human habitation since the first Homo sapiens appeared on earth. There are similar caves around the world where man lived during the initial ten thousand years of his existence.

So far archaeologists have found little except the most primitive tools. For example limestone pieces of rock that have been ground flat on the surface so rudimentary grains could be hammered and rubbed between them to make flour. No weapons or artifacts have been discovered, but they dig patiently month after month and have no idea what lies ahead. They did find a couple of primeval skeletons.

Adonis was the first man to rediscover the cave and attract the interest of professional archaeologists. As a result, Indiana and

Pennsylvania universities became interested and started their excavations.

That autumn, on the way back to France, I saw the prime minister. We had a whisky and an interesting chat while Christopher was entertained by the staff. As usual, Ambassador Petros Molyviatis, Caramanlis's political and diplomatic counselor, was present and interpreted. Costa not only has bad hearing but his knowledge of English has dwindled. He looked fine and fit though.

I said many people seemed concerned about what they see as a growing feeling of hostility toward the United States. He commented: "Bilateral relations between the United States and Greece do not present any problems. But these relations are in turn influenced by the Greek-Turkish dispute. The dispute perforce involves the United States as an ally of both countries no matter what it prefers.

"In its efforts to save Turkey as an ally, the United States does things which cause a negative reaction to the Greek problem. There is after all an old principle in life that a friend of my enemy is my enemy. There is a psychological bitterness here toward the United States, not hostility."

He said Carter's policy toward Greece stirs up a bigger reaction than Ford's. The U.S. administration made big but avoidable mistakes. These provoked indignation. "And it is I who will have to pay for this because everybody knows I am for America," he concluded.

He said: "Reintegration of Greece into NATO is an indication of the incoherence of the alliance. As a principle it is inconceivable that an alliance should not seek new members. It is inconceivable to put conditions on a country's reentry into an alliance.

"In 1977 we asked to be reintegrated. General Haig and General Dovas, our principal armed forces leader, had come to terms on conditions. The formula was approved by the other allies. But

Turkey vetoed it. In order to overcome Turkey's veto, General Haig modified the original agreement in a manner unacceptable to us.

"The United States and the other allies are trying hard to save Turkey. The arms embargo was lifted. The allies are again collecting money for the sake of NATO but allow Turkey to weaken the alliance by vetoing Greece's reentry. Is there any sense to that? Can Turkey be of any use to NATO without Greece as an ally serving as the connecting link to the other allies?"

Caramanlis said: "The Turks have a kind of schizophrenic position on Greece. They have a superiority complex which derives from the grandeur of the Ottoman Empire when Turkey ruled Greece for centuries. But now they have an inferiority complex as well, vis-à-vis the present situation. Turkey is one hundred years behind us in terms of social and economic development. Both complexes affect Greece more than any other country."

He told me his recent trip to western Europe had disappointed him greatly. There was no evidence of any willpower nor any policy left in a single country — not in France nor Germany nor England. He was very pessimistic. He said the West was going to lose Greece in one or two years if its present policy continues. And if they lose Greece, what on earth will they be able to do with Turkey?

As he talked he became more and more angry. It was almost hysteria. He said: "Everybody is against me but I am the most pro-Western and pro-American man in Greece. I cannot understand it."

Made a brief visit to Belgrade en route to Paris. Stayed with Eagleburger, his wife, and two handsome little boys. Christopher was carefully isolated from Chaka. Incidentally, Henry Kissinger had been there about a month before and told Larry there were two countries in which he would never dare to get out of a plane if it were forced down because he wouldn't be able to leave alive. One was Iran and the other Greece.

Had a very pleasant lunch with Djilas, Stephanie, and Aleksa, their son, who has just finished military service. Stephanie saw to it that Christopher got double his usual serving. Milovan told me: "Two years in prison is good. A long time is bad. It destroys the nerves. But it is not bad for a political or spiritual man. You can test yourself and your own possibilities. War is serious as a testing power but it is less complex. You are alone in prison when you are in solitary confinement. You are not exposed to accidents as you are in a war."

I asked him if he feels that he is free now that he is out of prison although not allowed to leave the country. He said: "If you are not allowed out of the country and you are not allowed to be able to do what you want — as I want to write and publish for my people — I see that there is no great difference except that I have my family around me and the circumstances are somewhat more pleasant."

Djilas recalled to me that he had done one term under the Royal Dynasty as a Communist and two terms, or nine years, as an anti-Communist under the present regime. In the first term under Tito, he was psychologically and emotionally very tense. He was not yet completely disconnected from his former colleagues, in his subconscious at any rate. This made for a good deal of nervousness. And it was difficult for him. "But when the second term came," he said, "I was quite calm and could continue for the rest of my life if necessary. I was free. I had resolved my own problems. I broke off subconscious contact with former colleagues. I never felt so free in all my life.

"A warden said to me once: 'You hate us.' I replied: 'No, I'm indifferent to you.' "

After the second term, he felt himself a larger, freer person. He was allowed to write and publish abroad but not to publish in his own country. He could travel inside Jugoslavia but not outside of the country. And people whom he had known were afraid to be seen with him because he was closely followed by the police. "Therefore I was isolated — but I did not feel alienated from life. I had developed a spiritual maturity. I felt like a hermit in the desert. I lived with my thoughts. I counted the seasons both after my imprisonment and during my second term instead of counting the days.

"Prison exists in every man psychologically. To be alone, to be oppressed, to fight. I feel guilty about my son. I feel responsible for going to prison when he was a small boy. But morally I had to go. When I went to prison, I thought about my son. I thought for him it would be better if I made a compromise by maneuvering my position. And the regime sent me a message suggesting a compromise but I refused." The message had been conveyed by Vlado Dedijer, whom he detests and thinks is crazy anyway. Vlado recently announced in the newspapers that his second boy, who committed suicide, had in fact been murdered by the CIA.

Djilas said the countries which can not be called prison countries are those of western Europe, the United States, Canada, and Australia. None of them are absolutely free and they all have some oppressive elements, but these are minor. Jugoslavia is different for different people.

Djilas said Jugoslavia today is better for the poor peasants than before the war, but not for the rest of the people. Prince Paul was right to say that without Tito Jugoslavia would not exist today. It would have been torn apart during the war or by the Soviet Union in 1948. But in many ways Jugoslavia now is less free than during the prewar period. He added: "Our greatest weakness is that we are not a juridical country now. Before the war there were certain legal rights which were made clear. The system was less arbitrary then than now." He said that he could live anywhere but he prefers to live in Jugoslavia. "This is my country," he added. "Still when I am here, I can do more for my people than anywhere else. I see my conflict with my former comrades more as a conflict between spiritual thought and violent action than between two political ideas."

He said that suffering does not — as Solzhenitsyn says — make a man more gentle. It provokes men to violence and excess. However, if he had not been alone in his first imprisonment and had been pressed to capitulate, he probably would have been different when he came out. Since he had been in solitary confinement he resolved to go to the end if necessary. During the second term, he reentered prison with "better equipment" for what faced him. He concluded: "Now I am less interested in fighting. I am more interested in meditation than I was a few years ago." We left Belgrade at 7:00 A.M. for the long drive to Trieste. The weather soon turned horrible — real November. Christopher was most unhappy. Nor was he made any more cheerful when I took him for a walk to a restaurant along the Trieste wharf where he could have a stretch and watch me eat (I had bribed my way to get him a luncheon in a small village restaurant in Slovenia). A thunderstorm broke out, dumping cold rain on him as he shivered with fright from thunder and lightning.

We took off for Desenzano, a pleasant little town on Lake Garda. It was a cold, misty drive but we halted in Soave, not far away, where Christopher had a remarkably good lunch. It's nice to be back in "Europe" where they don't kick dogs on principle. We went for a long walk after arriving at Lake Garda and I was horrified to see how nazified the place seems to have become. Almost every other house was guarded by a huge, savage German police dog. Christopher trotted by unconcerned, assuming (quite erroneously) that I would protect him if they managed to jump over the inadequately high fences that contained them. I was impressed by one street in the little village called Via General A. Papa. I would like to have him married off historically to Saint Mama, in whose honor the smallest church on Spetsais has been built.

Back in Paris I had a long talk with Bobbie de Margerie, French ambassador to Madrid and a close friend of Giscard d' Estaing. He said the Spanish king Juan Carlos was even surprised himself at the political ability he had developed since Franco's death. Although my pal, foreign minister Count Motrico, had assumed he was going to become prime minister after the fall of Arias, the Fascist predecessor, he did not realize that the king regarded him as an older intellectual who was a kind of tutor. He felt uncomfortable dealing with a man from another generation and wanted someone approximately his own age. That is why he chose Suarez.

Bobbie thought Santiago Carrillo, the Communist party leader, and Juan Carlos were perhaps the two most adroit figures in present day Spain. Carrillo is smart and appealing despite his murderously brutal civil war record. The reason he chose the alias "Giscard" under which to live during his long exile in France was that when he came as a refugee in 1939, he went to Clermont-Ferrand, simply opened a telephone directory and then with his eyes shut, put his finger on a name on a page. The name was Giscard. When the French president Valéry Giscard d'Estaing visited Madrid, he and Carrillo laughed about this accidental similarity in names.

Our year wound up with a small Christmas in Brittany where Christopher and I visited my old friend Rosane de Clermont-Tonnerre. She has four children but only two were there: Rénaud, her twenty-nine-year-old eldest son, and his wife, a great-niece of the Comte de Paris, claimant to the nonexistent French throne; and Gilles and his fiancée. It was a nice, cozy, family party.

Rosane has a *manoir* not far from Lanmeur, which is called the Manoir le Goasmelquin. It is a sixteenth-century house, rather rambling but very pretty, with two small buildings and a chapel next to it, and set on about thirty-five or forty acres of land. It is lovely country with huge trees. One of her ancestors had brought over a sequoia from California but it was cut down by her grandmother, who feared it might blow over in one of the frequent storms and fall on the house. We were still burning redwood logs in the fireplaces those cold days. Another of her ancestors had been French consul in New Orleans before the American Civil War and brought back a good deal of Louisiana furniture which is still there.

I did a great deal of walking with Christopher, exploring the countryside and the River Douron, which starts as a brook on Rosane's place and becomes a trout stream a little further down after a village called Pont Menou.

It was snowing heavily when we arrived in Brittany and it rained steadily for the first two days, much to Christopher's distress. However, Christmas was cold, sunny, gleaming, and much appreciated by all of us.

 Back in Paris I had a long talk with former president Richard Nixon in his hotel suite at the George V. He was on his way through, returning from a brief trip to the Ivory Coast. He had stayed on to make final arrangements for the publication and syndication of his new book on foreign policy. Christopher had to wait outside with aides. Although he was well treated by Nixon's staff, I had told him how Lyndon Johnson played with Benjamin Beagle. Christopher intends to vote Democratic.

Nixon was very friendly. He looked well although puffy in the face. He doesn't seem to have gained weight around the middle and has scarcely a single gray hair. He told me he had given up playing golf over a year ago. There was no point going on because he could never get any better, only worse.

For an ex-president I must say he travels well. It is all done by commercial planes but he has quite a gang with him. Lieutenant General Vernon Walters, retired deputy chief of the CIA, is his traveling companion, along with a whole batch of aides and Secret Service men, all housed at the George V.

We talked some about foreign affairs. Nixon thinks it is a good thing to have an independent country like France in the alliance. The French don't always accept everything we want just the way we want it; nevertheless they have been extremely useful because, fundamentally, they share our ideas and they know how to act quickly on their own.

If France took a fairly independent and different line from us in the wake of the Afghanistan situation, this was understandable because they have a much greater dependence on imports and exports than the United States. Our foreign trade is only two and a half percent of our entire trade and we could shrug it off if it disappeared. That is not the case with any European country. The French and Germans were lukewarm about boycotting the Olympics. The British, on the other hand, took a great risk by following our line in order to reestablish their "special relationship" with Washington even at the risk of somewhat jeopardizing their close link to Europe. The Germans were in a touchy situation right on the frontier of the Soviet bloc.

We finally turned to Afghanistan and Iran. I asked Nixon what he would do about them if he were sitting in the White House today. He acknowledged that the situation in Pakistan is very poor. He thinks Carter made a great mistake in not trying to behave more effectively with Pakistan. There is certainly a danger the country may disintegrate as a result of Russian or Indian pressures.

He personally believes the Russians did not go into Afghanistan primarily for any of the reasons cited by most commentators. Afghanistan was not a nonaligned country when the Russians moved in during January. It was to all intents and purposes a Soviet-aligned country. The government had been put in by the Russians and there were plenty of Russians around Afghanistan. But a counterrevolution was preparing to throw out the government. This was one thing the Russians could not tolerate — the idea of a successful counterrevolution in any place that called itself Communist.

Until the Afghan invasion, the Soviet Union had never used

its troops to agress upon foreign soil outside the Communist bloc. It preferred to use surrogate Communist armies like Cuban soldiers or East German soldiers in various parts of Asia and Africa. But it considered the threat of a counterrevolution in Afghanistan so strong that it decided to move in by itself and crush the opposition once and for all although it knew there were risks involved. However, these risks appeared to diminish when the United States showed that it was willing to stand by and not use force in Iran after the taking of American hostages.

It is clear that the Russians are going to have and hold Afghanistan. There is nothing anybody is going to be able to do about it. Things like boycotting the Olympic Games make no impression on the Russians although they get irritated. And it is pretty hard to imagine any kind of economic boycott that would press them to withdraw. What seems more likely to happen is that Moscow will eventually consolidate its position in Afghanistan and that gradually the world will accept this and the crisis will fade away. Then, perhaps at a later date, the Russians will either move by encouraging Baluchistan's separation from Pakistan and Iran or by threatening to cut off oil supplies in the Persian Gulf so that Japan and Europe are deprived.

The big thing to remember about the Russians is that they want the fruits of war without war itself. They would like to cut off sources of raw materials from the western world and Japan — and not only petroleum, but also various precious minerals such as uranium and titanium. They are fighting a kind of economic war which is not war. The only way for the West to face up to this is by getting militarily stronger than it is now. We must at least keep strategic nuclear parity with the Soviet Union. And we must work in closer harmony on nonnuclear defenses. If this is done, war is not going to come about. Otherwise, one by one, various friendly allied countries may be blackmailed into making concessions to the Soviet Union. A nuclear strength that really frightens the Russians and an indication of the willpower to use it if necessary is the only answer.

Furthermore, there has to be an economic revitalization in the United States and in the western world. To a large degree these two matters are linked. You cannot have economic revitalization without having access to adequate supplies of raw materials in world markets.

It is also absolutely necessary to make it clear that any option remains open to the United States and the NATO governments. In other words, we should never tell the Russians ahead of time either what we will do or what we won't do under given circumstances. The latter is even more important than the former. Eisenhower used to say that the one absolute imperative was to never let your opponent know what you will not do. If he knows that, he will move into the areas that aren't covered by any threat of what you will do.

There is no doubt that the free world has a much better ideology, and that it appeals to many more people than communism. Moreover, it is a far more efficient economic system. Look at Soviet agriculture. But this ideology must be shown to contain its own vigor. It requires leadership and that means, above all, American leadership.

If we are not seen to be aware of these things and to be prepared to act with sufficient resolve, we are going to be increasingly on the defensive throughout the world.

In March, before leaving for Greece, we spent three days at Château Lafite (about an hour from Bordeaux, in the Pauillac) with Marie de Rothschild, her son Eric, and his girlfriend. Eric now runs the Lafite wine property for the family. It is a happy hunting ground for Christopher, who has been there several times. All the other guests were English or Austrian Rothschilds or their spouses.

It was an interesting and agreeable weekend, with marvelous food and superb wines. We toured the entire Lafite winemaking establishment and also visited Château Latour and Château Mouton-Rothschild, thus touching base at three of the select five *premier cru* wineries of the claret area.

Lafite is a big property, with ninety-five acres of vineyard. One can approximately calculate, according to Eric, that ten vines produce one litre of wine. One hectare produces about two thousand five hundred litres.

Lafite, apart from its regular wine, produces a less superior quality called Carruades, mixed from the young wines not considered up to scratch. We had an excellent specimen of this from 1966.

The thousands of barrels in which the wine is stored in the *chais*, or sheds, are all of oak and last only one year. The growers are increasingly worried about finding enough oak for future years.

The huge vats, or *cuves*, in which initial fermentation starts are also oak but Latour has installed a new set made of stainless steel since the vineyard was purchased as an investment by the English Cowdrays a few years ago. Latour makes an equivalent of Carruades called Les Ports de la Tour.

I read two and a half books on wine during the weekend and it is a very special, somewhat contrived form of writing. Authors talk of a "big" wine or a "severe" wine. It is an enormously complicated business and involves large investments and great gambles on each year's weather, rainfall, and temperatures. There is also the risk of disease, like the phylloxera which slowly destroyed the area last century until it was revived with new vines from California. It takes an average of at least ten years for a new wine to mature. Eric says the corks in Bordeaux are longer than in other wines because, unlike cognac, claret ages in the bottle. For long-aging wines the corks must be changed about every twenty-five years.

Lafite is a local word for "height" just as *Mouton* derives not from "sheep" but from *motteau* or "little hill."

A vine lives eighty to one hundred years, then must be replaced after the land has lain fallow a decade. The entire Pauillac is really more or less reclaimed or filled-in land, largely arid and heavily pebbled but, for reasons of location, soil, and chemistry, ideal for wine.

Wine goes back to the third millennium B.C. In the poem of Sumerian Gilgamesh a temple harlot serves wine. Dionysus was the Greek god of wine. Homer praised it; Noah planted a vineyard on Mount Ararat. Horace, Anacreon, Aeschylus, Euripedes, Sappho, Socrates, and Plato all celebrated wine. *The Rubáiyát of Omar Khayyám* repeats its virtues over and over. Hafiz worships it.

In the seventeenth century the blind Benedictine monk and cellar master, Dom Perignon, introduced corking and thus, by retaining the bubbles, virtually invented champagne. The Duc de Richelieu, who died at ninety-four, credited his habit of drinking Lafite as the guarantor of his famous sexual vitality to the end.

The principal Lafite grapes are Cabernet-Sauvignon (the biggest share) and Merlot. Bordeaux's area is the largest French wine region, with over two hundred thousand acres of vineyard — more than double Burgundy's. In 1973 the Bordeaux area produced more than sixty million cases.

Claret is the English name for a pale red wine from Bordeaux which the British started to import in the twelfth century. The Haut Médoc uses the longest corks of any wine. A bottle of Bordeaux contains three-fourths of a liter. A magnum is two bottles; a double magnum, four; a jeroboam, six; an imperial, eight.

There are some châteaux in the Bordeaux region that go back for years, like Château d'Issan which dates back to the twelfth century. But in the Pauillac and Médoc regions most are late eighteenth or nineteenth-century buildings. There are over two thousand castles in the Bordeaux area. Bordeaux was under the English crown from 1230 to 1453 and was almost the only wine supplier for Britain. In the early fourteenth century about half of its annual one hundred ten thousand bottles were sent there.

The 225-liter cask *(barrique)* of Bordeaux was specially designed for English boats which carried about fifty tuns at a time. One tun equalled four *barriques*. Beer was wholly banned from medieval and Renaissance Bordeaux. After the British were expelled from France, Dutch entrepreneurs moved into the Bordeaux wine trade.

XVI   Christopher and I took off for Spetsais in March 1980. It was to be our final trip, the last spring of our deeply affectionate shared life. We started off in the usual chaos of mixed canine emotions, Christopher straining at the leash to get into our Volkswagen from the moment he saw his own suitcase loaded, and then settling resignedly into his corner, half under the front seat beside me.

We had a pleasant trip across Italy, entering through the Mont Blanc tunnel from France and spending the first night at an Italian ski resort nestled up against the Alps. The second day we drove to Bologna and, before a brief sightseeing tour, lunched at the Papagallo, a restaurant I had not been in for years. It is very highly reputed in Italy. They were exceptionally nice and gave Christopher an excellent lunch which he devoured with his customary greed and speed.

Then we drove on through Tuscany past Florence and Perugia to Assisi, which is really one of the loveliest small towns in the world. We were lucky enough to arrive at the entrance to the city just as a new hotel was opening its doors for the first night and they welcomed us with great hospitality. Assisi is beautifully made. Quite apart from the famous basilica where Saint Francis of Assisi is buried — which comprises two separate churches, one on top of the other, decorated with the famous frescoes by Cimabue and Giotto — the place is a wonderfully preserved medieval treasure.

The tomb of Saint Francis is a rather gruesome thing because his body was exhumed about three generations ago and reburied in a new monstrosity inside the basilica. But the view across the Umbrian countryside is magnificent and the frescoes are superb. We wandered around and ate in various little restaurants. To my great pleasure Christopher was welcomed wholeheartedly everywhere with the animal-loving spirit of Saint Francis. I even took him just inside the entrance of the thirteenth-century cathedral. This has a magnificent external facade but inside it has been restored in an onerous seventeenth-century style. The principal square of the city, which features a Roman temple of Minerva (later turned into a church) is splendid.

From Assisi we drove around Perugia, stopping to sightsee, and then down to Naples where we stayed as the guests of Admiral and Mrs. Harold Shear. Their villa, which has been used by the NATO commander in chief, south, ever since the post was created in 1951, is extremely comfortable.

Shear is a great admirer of Admiral Rickover, now eighty, and was one of his "colts" in nuclear submarines. He is the first Navy man in his family but for almost three hundred years they've been seafarers from Shelter Island, New York: commanding whalers, clippers, and merchant ships. Of modest financial circumstances, he fished and harpooned, clammed and trapped as a boy, to help finance his parents and his schooling. In his early teens he was sneaking up on basking swordfish (and occasional sharks), and stabbing them with his harpoon attached to a barrel by a rope. He sold his fish to New York's Fulton Street fish market at fifty cents a pound for swordfish, then a good price. He trapped skunks; shot deer, ducks, and geese; cut ice from the local pond to freeze his fish for transport in crates; and at the same time managed to educate himself. A splendid American story.

Shear is heavy-set, with a serious face but gentle manner, and filled with energy. He apparently sleeps only about five and a half hours a night. No matter when he goes to bed, he arises at dawn and jogs from three to six miles. He is a simple, nice man who reads his papers in the dining room of his ornate NATO house because the lamps elsewhere are too bad. When they retire to Maryland's eastern shore where they have bought a place, he is determined to renew his passion for fishing and bird-shooting, to saw wood, and to grow crops on his farm.

Shear and his charming wife left after we were there only one day because they were taking a trip home, carrying a lot of their personal belongings along. The admiral is retiring about six or seven months early because he is so frustrated by his unsuccessful efforts to heal the dispute between Greece and Turkey. But we remained on in the house for two and a half more days. Christopher enjoyed this lapse in the daily routine of travel which allowed him to do a lot of walking.

We also had a chance to do some sightseeing from Naples. A Navy car, provided by the admiral's office, took us one day to Herculaneum, then on down to Sorrento for lunch, and then to Pompei. Herculaneum was destroyed in A.D. 79 by the same eruption from Mount Vesuvius that smothered Pompei. The buildings in the small town, a commercial city on the Bay of Naples, show how a busy, industrious life was suddenly halted by this natural disaster. Everything was preserved under a blanket of lava, ashes, and mud that was spread across the borders of the Bay of Naples by a tidal wave.

I don't happen to like Sorrento much and it is a tedious drive getting there, along a narrow curving road. But Pompei has always fascinated me — rather more than Herculaneum. Christopher, who must have been getting quite an education for a member of the canine species, enjoyed the ancient odors of the city, where we visited the homes and gardens of prosperous inhabitants and even wandered into the lupanar, or brothel — it was the first time he had sniffed one of those.

From Naples we drove across Calabria and down the Adriatic coast to Brindisi. We were stuck there an extra day because our ferry was held up by a strike. This allowed time to walk Christopher around and to pay a visit to the splendid fish market along the wharf. In the evening, it was jammed with Mediterranean riches — large red snappers, octopus, clams, oysters, grey mullet, red mullet, squid, and other gleaming fish, large and small, whose species I did not recognize. We also strolled to my favorite little square where the Appian Way ends in Italy — only to resume across the Adriatic Sea in Albania, heading on toward Istanbul.

When we finally took off for Patras, I had the usual trouble with the Greek crew of the ferry which replaced the strike-bound Italian boat. As soon as we got through the tedious red tape that Greek bureaucracy always manufactures when given the chance, we climbed a stairway and were surrounded by ships' officers and stewards announcing that Christopher had to go to a special kennel section. I have often been warned against these kennels and told they are centers of contagion for sickness. As usual, I managed to get Christopher into the cabin and promptly hid him under my raincoat on the bed.

He played his role magnificently. Three times during the twenty-four-hour voyage, stewards came into the room searching for him. Each time he lay absolutely still and silent. They couldn't detect him, hiding flat and motionless beneath my rain-coat. He was exceedingly disciplined and wasn't able to relieve himself at all. The only food I managed to give him was a couple of horrible ham sandwiches which he gobbled with gusto. I gave him a little water to drink out of a glass. Yet, he survived well and once we were ashore at Patras he resumed his natural peeing habits. It was pretty late by the time we disembarked and got through the complicated series of Greek customs and formalities. So, instead of proceeding on to Athens, we holed up in a hotel in the new city of Corinth.

We arrived in Athens at the end of March, dropping Christopher at Spetsais while I spent the weekend attending the Onassis Foundation Awards ceremonies. The two prizes of $100,000 each were presented to Harold Macmillan, eighty-six-year-old former prime minister of Britain and principal mover in the committee to preserve the Acropolis, and to Madame Veil, first president of the European Parliament. The ceremony was held in the old Greek Parliament which is now a museum.

It is a lovely building and comes to life when there are people actually making use of it. It was jam-packed with participants and spectators. We, the members of the jury, and officials of the foundation sat on a stage. In front of us President Tsatsos, chief of state, sat alone, flanked by a naval aide. In the front row of spectators were Christina Onassis, daughter of the man who set up the foundation as a memorial to his son, and Prime Minister Caramanlis, as well as cabinet members and diplomats.

Madame Veil read a long but eloquent speech in excellent French. She is a heavy-set woman who is clearly very brave as well as intelligent. She managed to survive the rigors of the Auschwitz Nazi concentration camp in which she was incarcerated as a French Jewess from Alsace. When she had finished, after having stated some blunt truths about the necessity of defending democracy, old Macmillan limped up to the dais and stood before the microphone.

He was stooped but his voice rang out loud and clear. With only a few scribbled notes he managed to give a remarkable and poetic speech about the debt owed to classical Greece by the western world. He never missed a single word or phrase; it was a magnificent and moving performance. His only difficulty seems to be bad eyesight. His voice is strong and vigorous.

After the ceremony we had an official lunch, which a few of us preceded by drinks with Macmillan. He likes a couple of martinis before each meal and they seem to reinvigorate him — like refueling a jet airplane. That afternoon we had a meeting of the Onassis Foundation jury to discuss the next prizes.

In the evening we dined at the presidential (formerly the royal) palace. Tsatsos was charming. It was a formal occasion and we had all worn black ties but the atmosphere was extremely cordial. When Caramanlis arrived he came up as soon as he spotted me and pried me away from the group with which I was chatting. He said he had at last decided to go ahead with my original idea of a Whole Earth Museum. He has approved a project for building three museums in one complex, the principal one featuring Greek history and art from the very earliest moment of the Proto-Helladic period until today. He asked if I would stay on an extra day to come and see him. I agreed to do so.

Rather to my surprise, Tsatsos told me all the furniture in the presidential palace is still the property of exiled King Constantine and not of the Greek state. He pointed to a sofa in the anteroom in which we were gathering before dinner and said: "For example, that belongs to the king." He told me that around 1960 the Bavarian government had sent back to Greece the royal crown and other royal regalia that King Otho, first ruler of modern Greece, had taken away with him when he was kicked out in 1862.

The next evening I had drinks with Macmillan again before we went off to another dinner given in the honor of the two laureates. Macmillan did not seem overtired from his exertions. His usual two martinis picked him up. He was talking about the speechmaking proclivities of John Foster Dulles, the late American secretary of state. He said: "Foster used to give a press conference every day. Then on Sunday he would read the sermon in his Presbyterian church. He couldn't keep his mouth shut."

Returned promptly to Spetsais and Christopher. We spent a three-day Easter weekend which was marked by dreary, biting cold. The latter came as quite a surprise because just before Good Friday the weather had been superb; warm enough to swim.

It was especially sad because Greeks treat Easter as by far the most important holiday. Everybody cooks lamb on a spit out-of-doors and also *koukouretzi*, a kind of tripe and liver sausage, rather like French *andouillettes*. Another feature of the Greek Easter is hardboiled eggs, dyed red. For some reason they only use that color, unlike other Orthodox countries.

The third unique feature of Greek Easter is the continual noise coming from firecrackers, cap pistols, and any other gunpowder. I don't know why the festival should be celebrated that way but it starts before Good Friday and continues on after Sunday. Maybe because the 1821 revolt was sparked by a priest at Eastertime. Poor Christopher is totally terrified during this entire period because the noise of a gun or anything like it is the most frightening thing on earth to him. He was trembling constantly and didn't even eat most of the good food placed before him.

A few afternoons later, I took a long walk over the mountain with Christopher. I never saw Spetsais look so lovely although the weather was cold, with occasional drizzling. Normally in summertime the only green spot on the island is the pine forest region on the higher parts of the mountain. But now the entire island is green and lush. Every field is thick with green, growing, wheat. There are poppies, huge clusters of yellow daisies, and thousands of wild irises, a delicate little flower but the usual purple in color. Shepherds here and there are shearing their fat sheep. Everywhere is tranquility.

Dined one evening with Christopher at the home of Sture and Cleo Linner. Sture has been working for the United Nations a good thirty years. He had just come back from a couple of months in Cambodia and North Vietnam. He is obviously a competent and courageous fellow as well as very nice and extremely intelligent. He knows excellent modern and classical Greek. Indeed, he translated some of the poems of George Seferis into Swedish so the Swedish Academy could give proper consideration to his nomination for the Nobel Prize for literature.

Sture was one of the closest assistants of Dag Hammarskjöld when he was secretary-general of the United Nations. He was with Hammarskjöld in the Congo and was scheduled to go along with him and one other aide on his fatal flight from the Congo. At the last minute, Hammarskjöld decided it would be a good idea to leave somebody behind in case of any accident. In that way Sture's life was spared. He said that Hammarskjöld at the time was preparing the nomination of Martin Buber for the Nobel Prize for literature.

He talked a lot about Hammarskjöld's death. It is still an unsolved mystery. The secretary-general flew from Katanga (Shaba) to Leopoldville (now Kinshasa) and then, after a brief halt, on toward Salisbury, Rhodesia. At that time Southern Rhodesia and Northern Rhodesia (now respectively Zimbabwe and Zambia) were united under one British governor general. The governor general, Lord Alport, was extremely unhelpful in investigating the crash after it occurred. The plane came down over Rhodesian territory some distance from Salisbury. Sture said it had been shot at and hit earlier in the flight, probably over Katanga. But the damage was hardly noticeable. He has a suspicion that the plane was actually shot down before it finally crashed.

One great mystery was the disappearance of the briefcase Hammarskjöld had with him. It only contained a few uninteresting and unimportant papers and some of his work on the translation of Buber but the briefcase has never been found.

Sture indicated that the Union Minière, a holding company which controls the copper mines in Katanga, was eager to have the province break off from the Congo and become independent, under its own tutelage. Tshombe, then boss of Katanga, was the stooge of the Belgian company. But another company — a huge British concern — was the holding company of the Union Minière. Linner seems to believe that some kind of arranged assassination occurred and that either the Belgian company or the British company was secretly involved. He gives the impression that he believes London pressure was behind Alport's reluctance to help investigate the crash. The Swedes are deeply concerned about this and are still actively looking into the case.

He talked about Cambodia and North Vietnam. He always keeps in mind Harold Nicholson's advice to his son who was going off on an assignment to Egypt: "Don't ever expect to understand what the Orientals are telling you. You are much too stupid. Just be sure that they understand what you say." This is the practice Sture employs with Vietnamese and Cambodians. He met a very high-ranking North Vietnamese in Hanoi on his most recent trip. The man said: "You must be a Communist."

Linner was astonished. "Certainly not," he replied. "I am no kind of a Communist. I oppose them all — Russian communism, Chinese communism, Titoism, and the lot."

The Vietnamese was astonished. "But why are you so interested in helping us out and also the Cambodians?" he asked.

Linner replied: "If someone is run over and seriously injured by a truck, you don't ask him what party he belongs to before you start helping him."

The Vietnamese said: "I never thought of that." From then on they were great friends.

That April we spent a long weekend with Paddy and Joan Leigh Fermor in Kardhamíli on the edge of the Mani. It is really a magnificent coast.

From Costa, opposite Spetsais, we drove along the east shore of the Gulf of Argos to Nauplia. I am fascinated to think that the Peloponnesos could spawn such people — both real and mythical — as Jason, who guided his Argonauts to the Black Sea, Agamemnon, Nestor, who led the second largest Greek fleet to Troy from Pylos, Hercules, and Atalanta, the fleetest runner of her day. It was also on the west coast of the Peloponnesos that the legendary River Styx flowed and Charon ferried dead passengers to their eternal home.

Nauplia was an important trading post at the head of the Argolic Gulf and was well-known under the Venetians. After Venice took Constantinople in 1204, in the Fourth Crusade, Nauplia fell to Geoffroi de Villehardouin and subsequently became an appanage of the dukes of Athens. From then on it kept bouncing around between the Byzantine Empire, the Venetians, and the Turkish Empire. In 1827 the first Greek parliament met there at the end of the Independence War and in 1828 it became the provisional seat of government. The first king, Otho of Bavaria, disembarked in Nauplia in 1833 and kept his government there a year.

Only a few miles away is Argos, which Homer described as "very thirsty." It is on a plain and was famed in ancient times for its horses. Less than seven miles south of Argos is the modern Miloi, an undistinguished little village on the site of ancient Lerna, where Hercules slew the Hydra.

From there to the capital, Tripoli, the largest town of Arcadia. It is an ugly town but very near the ancient Tegea, biggest of all the ancient cities on the plain of Arcadia. The Tegeans sent five hundred men to the battle of Thermopylae because it was a vassal state of Sparta. It was also the birthplace of Atalanta.

Arcadia is a pleasant area to motor through during late April, with its tall rugged mountains and green plains filled with wheat and shaggy, munching sheep; wheeling crows; jinking doves and gliding pigeons; its blossoming almond, Judas, and orange trees; and its groves of oak and cypress beneath the bleak, stern Parnon Mountains. I let Christopher out to run several times. A great many of the heights are still dominated by the ruins of strategically placed fortresses built over thousands of years, from Mycenaean to medieval, Frankish to Byzantine times and on to the Turkish era.

Climbed over the pass of Kaloyerikos descending into the plain of Asea, beyond which one first sees the high range of the Taygetus. As usual, we lunched on souvlakia in Megalopolis, a small town built near the ruins of the "Great City" which once was the capital of the Federated States of Arcadia. It was chosen as a site by the famous Theban general, Epaminondas.

The theater, built in the fourth century B.C., is supposed to have been the largest in all Greece, containing fifty-nine rows of seats holding twenty-one thousand spectators. Only the lowest tiers are now well preserved.

On to Andrítsaina, an attractive village with stone-built houses on the side of a mountain. Thence upward along a climbing mountain road to the ancient temple of Apollo Epikourios ("The Helper") at Bassae, almost four thousand feet up, atop Mount Kotilion. It is one of the most famous Greek temples and was relatively well preserved because of its inaccessibility. It is built of cold gray local limestone and overlooks a melancholy, austere landscape. The architect was Ictinus, who also built the Parthenon. It once had twenty-three famous marble slabs in its frieze showing battles between centaurs and Lapiths. However, these were stripped by nineteenth-century explorers, sold to the British government years ago, and placed in the British Museum.

A few years ago Bassae was badly shaken by earthquakes and has not yet been restored. The shaky pillars are shored up by wooden beams. Yet it is a lovely sight on the windy mountaintop, under rainclouds scudding overhead — a grim gray temple. The whole impression is as austere and forbidding as the landscape it looks down on. Even Christopher seemed awestruck.

Then proceeded to Messenia, the area of Greece along the southwestern part of the Ionian Sea where the Leigh Fermors live. Coming out of the highlands to Messenia is lovely. It is a sunny, warm, lush, lowland coastal area behind which rears the other flank of the harsh Taygetus mountains leading right up to jagged snow-streaked crags. Just outside Kalabáka, the provincial capital, we passed the general region where a Frankish army of the thirteenth century beat the Byzantine forces led by the Great Domestic of the Eastern Empire.

Messenia is one of the six ancient countries in the Peloponnesos. In the Homeric age it was dominated by the kings of Pylos, of whom the most famous was Nestor. In the eighth century b.c. it was conquered by Sparta. Many Messenians emigrated to Sicily where they captured a little town which is now the modern Messina.

Drove through Kalabáka to Kardhamíli — a splendid trip, starting along the seacoast and then climbing above it through endless olive groves and green fields sprinkled with flowers, and many cacti, with heavy prickled leaves, leaning over stone walls. Kardhamíli is a small village with an air of absolute repose, but it has suddenly been discovered by tourists.

Paddy and Joan first came to the area hiking over the Taygetus in the 1950s. In 1962 they bought their present plot of about six acres, mainly olive groves, along the coast with their own private beach. They drew up plans and then got an expert architect to go over them. They helped with the building and cement-mixing, then brought all their books and possessions from England. It is a gorgeous place, built of honey-colored local limestone in a kind of Greek style with arches like the cloister of a monastery. The bedrooms are exceptionally comfortable and the bathrooms modern. The sitting room is really magnificent. It has an almost Renaissance type of wooden ceiling divided into squares. There is also a special kind of earthquake-proofing around the top of the building. The sitting room is lined with books, including a marvelous reference library. There are also several extremely good paintings, some by their friend Nikos Ghika. The splendid fireplace was designed by Paddy from one he remembered from his travels in Persia.

Next to the main house is a smaller stone building where Paddy has his studio, bedroom, and bathroom. He works several hours every day on his books and has another fine library there. There is a third building, behind which is a home for the couple who act as gardener and cook-housekeeper.

A few notes about the Mani. Kardhamíli is at the northern frontier but does contain several of the square stone towers for which the whole Mani is famed. These were built by local families of some prestige, especially military ones, in order to have bases from which to destroy each other in continuing blood feuds. Paddy wrote a splendid book on the Mani which was published in 1958. He probably knows more about the area than anybody.

The Maniots are generally lean, dark, and very hairy. They are renowned as terribly fierce fighters. This is as it should be, I suppose, because the Mani seems to have been originally settled by the Spartans, who came in several waves. The Mani was Christianized only in the ninth century. Eventually refugees from barbarian invasions, and Cretans fleeing the wars resulting from their own clan system also moved into the area. The basic city is Areopolis. Areopolis derives from Ares, the Greek god of war. Originally it was named Tsimova, of Slavic derivation judging from the initial two letters, "ts," which are a Slavic syllable. Slavic invaders came right on down to the end of the Peloponnesos. There were also considerable settlements of Albanians driven southward by Turkish rulers.

Petro Bey Mavromichalis of Areopolis really started the Greek Independence War in 1821 by forming a force which spent its last night before the first big battle in Kardhamíli and the subsequent day captured Kalabáka.

When poor Maniots die they are given a solemn Christian burial but also a coin to pay Charon to ferry them across to the underworld. In the Mani there is always particular rejoicing when a son is born to a family. This means there is one more "gun" to help fight in the endless feuds. All male babies are called "guns." Girl babies are unwelcome, as in old Sparta. No parties or presents are given when a girl is born. They are regarded only as "gun-breeders." At death, there is mourning only for men, not women.

Most of the towers were built between the fourteenth and nineteenth centuries, constructed with thick walls to defend families or clans during their eternal quarrels. The most formidable belong to prominent clans and are built on high ground.

Took a long walk with Paddy, about eight miles across the mountain. Paddy, who is sixty-five but looks about forty-eight, is in splendid condition. In 1977 he and several friends — all in their sixties — went to the Himalayas and did a high climb with Sherpa porters from Ladakh.

Also strolled with Joan to the area just below the old acropolis of Kardhamíli, near several ruined towers and an old stone church owned by a madwoman. She keeps it locked and won't let the priest in. The path is thick with blackberry bushes. We talked with a charming old lady who gave us some roses. Practically everybody I saw had blue or blue-green eyes. As we were descending, the madwoman who owns the church came by. She looked extraordinary: short, wiry, bent, with an almost toothless mouth, and flaming eyes. She was ragged and dirty, wearing sandals and one sock, and leading a plump donkey. She stopped and chatted away, rolling her eyes ferociously, warning Joan, "The killers are on their way." I was interested to see a small truck loaded with coffins parked on the sole village street.

Paddy is the son of a British official in India. He never saw his father until he was five, nor really knew his mother until he was four — typical in the days of the British Empire. He was educated at King's School, Canterbury, but was thrown out at the age of sixteen for getting involved with a local girl. King's Canterbury was renowned for its teaching of the classics and languages. Paddy has an impressive talent for both.

One afternoon we drove to Tseria, another village with a Slavic name, high in the mountains above a very ferocious gorge. All the former Slavic invaders seemed to have remained around this area but they were swallowed amid the sea of Hellenism, leaving only occasional place names and blue eyes.

The last day we visited the pathetic little tombs of Castor and Pollux, the twins who accompanied Jason's Argonaut expedition to the Black Sea in search of the Golden Fleece. The graves one sees are just two rather short holes in the ground fenced off with an iron grill. Local tradition insists it is the twins. Personally I doubt it; they are also reputed to be buried in a Black Sea-covered town near Sukhumi, Soviet Georgia.

Departed on a magnificent day. We could hear the echoes of shots in the mountains, causing Christopher to tremble. Like all Greeks, the Maniots will shoot anything on sight and were having a great time hunting turtledoves on their northward spring migration.

It was a beautiful drive along a narrow road above the sea, winding in and out from the water to high mountains and down again. Gradually the rich, fertile Messenia dissolves into the rugged Mani of scrub oak, bushes, and rock, rock, rock.

Eventually reached Areopolis. It is a nice little town and the biggest in the deep Mani. Drove down the barren peninsula toward Cape Matapan, through villages containing many rugged towers of stone built by the Maniot people for their blood feuds.

Then turned back and eastward to Gytheion, a very pleasant seashore village. The water stretching in front of it was like a smooth mirror reflecting the intensely blue sky. Just outside the town, linked by a small causeway, is a tiny island called Marathonisi. This is where Paris and Helen spent their first night of connubial bliss after he stole her from her husband, the king of Sparta, and took her off to Troy. In Homeric days, the island was called Kranae.

Then northward toward Sparta. The road aims straight up at the snow-covered Taygetus range. Occasional hunters, with guns slung over their shoulders, wandered along the side of the road, searching for northward-bound doves. Once again, the land of green fields and blossoming white almond and red Judas trees on the hillside below the impressive Taygetus.

Gytheion was the ancient port of Sparta, just as it is its contemporary port now. It is the second largest town in Laconia, seat of Sparta itself. Hercules and Apollo are claimed to be the founders of Gytheion and the great Theban general, Epaminondas, tried unsuccessfully to besiege it.

Sparta, the capital of Laconia, is ugly and modern, but near unimpressive ruins of the ancient warlike city on the banks of the Eurotas River. Old Sparta had few magnificent public buildings and Thucydides rightly predicted that its remains would be scanty in the historical future. In olden days, it was a terrifying state, purely fascist. The top class was called Spartiate. The middle class was called Perioikoi. The Helots were at the bottom of the heap. Only the Spartiates were full citizens. They had a complicated form of government headed by two kings whose principal role was simply to command the army in battle. Probably not more than ten thousand Spartiates ruled all of Lacedaemon. Their lands were cultivated by the Helot slaves. The Spartans educated their children with strict discipline and in mass camps. At twenty, each Spartiate entered the army or the secret police. The only function of marriage seemed to have been to produce children — boys. The fathers kept living in their barracks. The Perioikoi were free men but had no rights as citizens. They were called up as hoplites, more or less the basic infantry of the army. The Helots were serfs and completely under the control of the Spartiates although they were many more in number. They worked on the estates of the upper class. Despite this rather grim system, Sparta's music and dancing at festivals were famous and there was a certain amount of other creative art.

Sparta of course defeated Athens in the Peloponnesian War and was thus the most powerful state in the whole Aegean area. But that didn't last long because the Greeks found Sparta an even more unpleasant master than Athens, and a coalition of other states defeated the Spartans and divided their subject territories.

Forbidding as ancient Sparta was, it had a magnificent location under the high, imposing, saw-toothed Taygetus, still covered in snow along the top at the end of April.

From Sparta to Mistra is only about five miles west. It is one of Europe's most lovely medieval cities, built on the side of a steep hill which terminates in a cliff and lies right below the crags of the Taygetus. On the peak above is an impressive fortress, first

built in 1259 by Guillaume de Villehardouin to protect the town
of Mistra from raiding Slavs who had established themselves in
the Taygetus on their way down to Cape Matapan.

Drove up the rear road toward the fortress and then walked the
rest of the way along a steep, rocky path strewn with sun-basking
lizards. The fortress had thick crenellated walls and a whole
series of defenses. The principal entrance was through a massive
stone gate. It fell into the Byzantine Empire's hands when Villehardouin was taken prisoner in 1259 at Pelagonia by Michael
Paleologos and bought his freedom by surrendering Mistra,
Monemvasia, and the Mani.

From 1349 on, the whole area was governed by the Despot of
Mistra who was generally either a son or brother of the Byzantine emperor. It finally fell to the Turks in 1460, and subsequently to the Venetians, back to the Turks, and eventually to
independent Greece.

During its fairly brief history as a medieval center, Mistra was
famous for its eminent leaders in the world of arts and letters. At
times it was even ahead of Constantinople itself in the development of ideas. Had Emperor Michael VIII not defeated their
army at Pelagonia, it might have remained for decades in Frankish hands. It was obviously rich and civilized and is one of the
few ruins of the Middle Ages where one can see surviving some
of the features of civilian life — like the houses of wealthy people
or the palaces of the ruler.

There is a lovely cathedral that was built in 1309. In the floor
is set the famous two-headed marble eagle that was a symbol of
Byzantium. This one probably commemorates the coronation in
Mistra of Emperor Constantine XI.

There are several charming fourteenth-century churches
with remnants of some marvelous frescoes. In the upper town,
between the main city and the fortress, is what was left of the
Palace of the Despots. It is very rare to have such an extensive
ruin of a civic Byzantine building. I found the most beautiful of

all the churches to be the Pantanassa, which is attached to a convent.

From Mistra back to Sparta where I had a quick glass of retsina and Christopher gobbled grilled steak. Then off for Tripoli, Nauplia, and home at last to Spetsais.

That was the final voyage of Christopher Doghead's education.

THREE ✿ "They Shall Not Know This is *Christopher*"

XVII Spring is the best season to start or end a great adventure because it is the season of hope and it is garlanded with beauty. There is nothing nostalgic about spring itself, much as we may distort it with our private sorrows. Of the latter I cherish one in particular, the sweet memory of my wife, Marina; the rest are but comparatively minor regrets than which nothing can be more remote.

As for Christopher, it is difficult for me to read his thoughts. He is a moody dog — by sudden, swift turns astonishingly gay and mischievous and then pensive, dolorously sad. His evident traits are inquisitiveness, a tendency to show off (above all by frisky gamboling or appallingly loud barks) yet, despite the appearance of bravado, he is not much on courage. But he is independent, true, loyal, and generally happy. I know he loves me. He sleeps on my bed and if I go for a long swim, he follows me along the shore, leaping from rock to rock, to be sure I am overcome by no dire fate. He is my protector and we desperately need each other.

A dog assumes the personality and characteristics of his master and this has been unusually true in the case of my best, last, and closest friend. He mirrors my most intimate moods, hidden from all other creatures. Therefore, as this night of May first descended (the night of Marina's birthday), and once again my mind contemplated the dreadful plan with which it had so long been occupied, he came up to me with that special, gentle silence which is his tender gift. He placed his head on my knee and regarded me with luminous, understanding eyes. I thought of Robert Burton and what he wrote in his distressingly beautiful *Anatomy of Melancholy:*

> If a man put desperate hands upon himself, by occasion of madness or melancholy, if he have given testimony before of his Regeneration, in regard he doth this not so much out of his will, as from the violence of his malady, we must make the best construction of it, as Turks do, that think all fools and mad men go directly to heaven.

Neither Turk nor fool nor mad myself, I reckon, but surely given to melancholia, a condition strangely enhanced and purified by the soft magnificence of the Aegean night now clasping us in its embrace.

I often wonder what man or woman able to contemplate death with any deliberation at an age when he or she must inspect its relative imminence, even if it be not self-inflicted, neither fears nor welcomes it because that person's life has been well lived. Few, I venture. A plate-glass window separates each of us from the past and present; and the future is unknown, if convincingly dismal and anonymous. The future's pane of glass is thick, dark, and opaque.

These thoughts cannot be even approximately shared with anyone, not even a trusting beagle with his head across your thigh and his eyes hypnotic with affection. How does one creature know what pain actually is to others? Do they bear it better or feel it less? Likewise, love, intimacy, hatred? Perhaps before dying it is desirable and useful to try to share the wisdom gained by one's brief and giddy period of existence.

I have never belonged anywhere. A Jew by lineage and pride, I am an atheist by credo and nonreligion. I am white by what is called race and American by three centuries of descent. Yet almost my entire adult life has been lived outside my country. My soul is in Greece, my mind is in France, my memory is in the United States. I married a Greek girl in Beirut; my daughter was born in Cairo; my son in Athens. My grandchildren were born in London and are English. What is left of my heart is entwined with that little palpitating heart of Christopher. Having long since resolved that I would outwit time and decrepitude before they joined to cripple me, how could I possibly leave behind my most trusting friend to mourn in a solitude he could not comprehend and that would never even remotely be understood or assuaged by others?

How could I conceive of Christopher's own diary had he written down his thoughts and recollections of our shared and poignant anniversary? "Is he sad? But we walk on the mountain and he has given me both good meat and sweet carrots and a fine bone so I feel happy. Only I wish he seemed so too. How can I amuse him and make him gay? But there is something bothersome in my mind as well. I don't know what it is. Ah, but it's fun to experiment with all these smells among the trees and flowers. Yes, there is the track of my enemy the hare. Fresh, rich, fragrant. I shall follow him with special cunning. He is a wily fellow because now his scent has suddenly disappeared. See, there is another tortoise. A strange, dank smell. Without real interest. But I shall go back to him, my friend. I have a feeling he needs me. That he is troubled. A pity, on such a splendid day. How fine to stretch my legs and creep along my belly through the brush. See how I frighten those big woolly sheep? What foolish creatures they are."

And so on. Maybe his thoughts are far more deep and sorrowful. I shall never know.

We descend. It has become full night as we work our way down the narrow, rock-strewn path from Y Khara. The moon sails westward but its luminosity is unneeded, thanks to the gleaming incandescence of the stars. Christopher skips lightly, sometimes running ahead, sometimes disappearing to the side only to emerge at my heels, sometimes trotting in front with his white tail pointing proudly toward heaven.

Back among the village streets, I follow him to our house

where, while he laps cold water from his yellow bowl, I sneak downstairs and get my shotgun. Although it is broken down and fitted in its leather case, I had carefully oiled and cleaned it only two days earlier. Now I extract eight number-six cartridges, twelve bore, and drop them in a pocket just to be doubly certain in case any have gotten damp. When I return for Christopher he looks suspiciously at the case in my hand but is comforted and reassured when he sees I wear only bathing trunks, an old bush jacket and moccasins — my usual garb for swimming or boating forays. And I carry my pink towel and his special ragged blue towel to reassure him.

We head to Vassili's tavern, beside the pier where our hired skiff is warped to a stanchion. I notice two sailors drinking ouzo with one of the island's few policemen, Yanni, a pleasant gruff fellow.

"The season's over," he says with a slight smile. "What do you expect to shoot with your gun?"

"Myself," I reply. The three roar with laughter.

"You won't need Christopher for that," says Mitso, one of the sailors. "The only thing poor Christopher can hunt is meatballs."

Again they laugh. Christopher looks offended. He growls; he doesn't like policemen.

We descend to the boat. Very carefully I lay my gun case on the thick, broad cork board I had had made for me by Nikolo, a carpenter, explaining I wanted it as a bulletin board in my downstairs office. Then Christopher takes his accustomed place in the stern, on the back seat, ears standing out in the breeze, parallel to his sweet face, eagerly watching as I fix the oars in their locks, haul up the heavy small anchor and its rusting chain, and shove into the smooth, lapping waters of the bay.

"*Yassou*," I shout to the trio of drinkers.

"God be with you," they reply.

As we creak steadily out of the Old Harbor and around Lighthouse Point, the moon hovers, radiantly bright, shining upon the

Peloponnesos and its bleak mountain ranges — the eternally life-less, waterless moon. Christopher sits watching me with eager attention as I swing backward and forward at oars which are awkwardly carpentered and too short. His eyes embrace me with innocence, love, and abiding faith.

Stars stare down, bright and bleakly confiding. They seem alive despite their extraordinary distance away in space and the incredible time it takes their light to reach us. While I labor with the clumsy oars I think again that the only time is now and that tomorrow is but a metaphor. The stars prove this by being real to us even though many at which we look with such admiration actually vanished in explosions centuries ago.

Slowly we lumber over the rippling sea, around the point and through the Spetsopoula channel. I think of that tricky Venetian fleet which in 1263 had been sent from nearby Nauplion, then the Most Serene Republic's principal Peloponnesian base, to the lit-tle Spetsais port we have just left. It lay in wait for a huge convoy of Genoese and Byzantine vessels, carricks, and great galleys escorted by long warships equipped with lateen sails, heading from Monemvasia to Constantinople and the Black Sea to trade for grain, furs, and gold. The Venetians detested their rivals from Genoa the Superb and held the Greek emperor, Michael VIII Paleologus, in contempt. Alerted by their spies, the Adriatic sailors and troops sprang like sea leopards upon their unprepared enemies and sank them but a few miles south of where we are.

For us it would be a long pull in a cumbersome craft. Already I am tired. The last few nights have been white nights because, as an aging man, I suffer increasingly from insomnia (as well as introspection). The combination made me suddenly realize with horror that in all my long life I had never done a single thing of which I could be genuinely proud: no act of true courage, gener-osity, sacrifice, or even pure kindness. It is appalling to contem-plate — which I did. After my dear wife, so filled with compas-sion, love and loyalty, had died, there was little encouragement to rectify that terrible lack. And now there is no time; only a matter of hours to be punctuated in the end by gentleness, heartbreak, cruelty, and terror.

Although Christopher is not an easy, fluent conversationalist he has an infallible knack for discerning when he is being told truth or falsehood. When I said in a low, soothing voice that something desperate awaited, he already knew it. I could see that he was slightly bewildered but retained utter confidence in me. He had, in his innocence, no fear of the dread prestige of peril. The sheer beauty of his trust, of his readiness to follow me anywhere, brought me anguish. It was as if he were saying in his own gentle way those terrible words of Job: "Though Thou slay me, yet shall I worship Thee, but I shall maintain my own way before Thee."

There is an eternally latent horror in human existence for the very reason that man created God in order to destroy Him, not vice versa. Christopher had had a good life — enthusiastic, generous, and tender. But I — apart from the blessing of Marina and the children — had wasted life, only tasting it, observing others. My sole accomplishment was now about to happen: a well-conceived death, fine dying.

With Christopher beside me, I would sink beneath the final waters of the soft Aegean to be swallowed by the universal cannibalism of the sea. We would placelessly perish and drift without a grave, borne on the invisible deep currents past rocks, sandbars, wrecked ships, amphorae, brothers to Mycenaean oarsmen, Phoenician merchants, Venetian traders, Genoese carrickmen, Byzantine slaves, the vast jars of Cretan wine dealers, and the bones of countless sailors who perished in the unending wars that inevitably sweep the world's loveliest sea.

"Look Christopher," I say as the creaking oars move us steadily through the strait between the islands where people always rumor the presence of sharks but rarely see them. "See how the little *merides* with their large friendly eyes peer up at the moon. See how they jump from the phosphorescent swirls when the thin *sarbanis* fangs at them with his long, saw-toothed beak. They are such dear little fish. Yet you love to eat them, fried by Jovita. You will walk on your two hindlegs just in order to get one and gobble him entirely, crisp and warm. Now here he is again, and you can't gobble him. The *sarbanis* is doing your job for you. And the *sarbanis* likes him raw."

We are now well around the point. Only a few lights gleam from the spaced-apart coastal dwellings on Spetsais and Spetsopoula. Far away one can see the brilliant arcs at the sterns of little *grigri* boats that are towed by caiques to the more distant shoals where, when the moon has set and cool darkness prevails, they will spread their nets in the eternal Mediterranean hope of a rich finny harvest. How little changes; and how much. Yet this remains the very pelvis of the world, its sexless womb, which has known, endured, survived so much and shown such relatively slight scars from this experience.

There is a certain excitement, I imagine, a joy to young death, leaping from an unexpected peak. That is not like the steady, drear immutability of old death, no matter how deliberately designed, heading with full consciousness and no carefree glee to dull eternity. I am at one with the endless procession of palsied septuagenarians with uncontrolled bowels and fitful tremors, followed to their designated graves by hordes of embarrassed mourners regarding the heedless carcasses or coffins.

Is predeath loneliness in any way different from the loneliness of life? Regard the innumerable stars, the relatively few clusters a human eye is capable of seeing. When I do so I know that of the four billion people now alive with me, at this last glimmer of personal time, there is only one creature to whom I can confide my secret thoughts: Christopher. He doesn't understand these thoughts, although he perceives their general tenor. Yet he looks at me with sympathy and helpless effort in his liquid eyes even though he is unable to join the endless recollection of my locked-in memories.

I row on and on, considering the pity I cherish for all condemned before, now, and hereafter: those of my forefathers I have known and am about to join (although we shall remain forever isolated from each other despite our shared sleep); those I quit and those who are yet to come. I have no self-pity, only regret, regret for the things I did not do, the legion of missed opportunities to accomplish acts of kindness, of charity, of compassion, and affection.

"Christopher, I shall quote to you a sermon on Death the Leveler by Dean John Donne and maybe if I change the name so you will hear a familiar ring, you will understand some of the solemn things you now face.

" 'It comes equally to us all, and makes us all equal when it comes. The ashes of an Oak in the Chimney are no Epitaph of that Oak to tell me how high or large it was; it tells me not what flocks it sheltered while it stood, nor what men it hurt when it fell.

" 'The dust of great persons' graves is speechless too, it says nothing, it distinguishes nothing: as soon the dust of a wretch whom thou wouldest not, as of a Prince thou couldest not look upon, will trouble thine eyes, if the wind blow it thither; and when a whirlwind hath blown the dust of the Churchyard into the Church, and the man sweeps out the dust of the Church into the Churchyard, who will undertake to sift those dusts again, and to pronounce, This is the Patrician, this is the noble flower, and this the yeomanly, this the Plebeian brain. So is the death of *Christopher* expressed. They shall not say, this is *Christopher*, not only not wonder that it is, nor pity that it should be, but they shall not say, they shall not know, This is *Christopher*.' "

Almost fifty years ago a medical journal listed in descending order the proportional reasons for suicide: madness, old age, illness, domestic trouble, love, poverty, misfortune, disgust, boredom with life, excessively weak or exalted character, remorse, fear of dishonor, laziness, delirium, jealousy, gambling, unemployment, pride, vanity, and mixed motives grouped together as "moral misery." This was a European analysis and certainly the causes of self-immolation vary greatly from generation to generation and place to place.

Double suicide, usually stemming from deep mutual love, has destroyed many men and women, several of them renowned. It is most frequent in Japan, which even has a precise name for it, *shinjo*. The analyst concludes that it was usually the woman who initially conceived the idea and urged her man to agree. Thus, the mistress of a French poet, fearing he would soon cease to love her because she was older than he, successfully persuaded him that they should die together. But feminine prompting was by no means always the case. When Marcus Junius Brutus lost the battle of Philippi in Macedonia, he slew himself with his sword; and his adored Portia promptly committed suicide in the hope of joining him in eternity. But double suicide with dogs is rarer.

History is speckled with occasions when stern-faced generals, defeated on the field of war, chose voluntary death: Hannibal, Hamilcar, Mithradates. Chinese emperors almost made it commonplace: Chaiou, Chung Ching, Kibin Ussenti, Tchbou Sin. According to Herodotus, the great pharaoh Rameses II killed himself on his hundredth birthday (although there is no trace of such immolation on his mummy in the Cairo Museum).

Age was more of a suicidal factor in ancient days than now when the elderly are cosseted by social security and welfare, or gathered in Kafkaesque *pensiones* to be preserved and babied into their graves. But in classical times the Greek island of Cos prescribed suicide as a legal requirement for anyone more than sixty years old. Many distinguished Romans, from Seneca to Atticus, deliberately ended their lives to avoid the torments and embarrassments of senility. Some scholars even say Emperor Diocletian committed suicide at Salona; not because of any guilty feelings about his cruel persecution of the Christians, but to escape decrepitude.

It is strange that the fewer the hours remaining of one's life the greater becomes the desire to terminate them; like a moth rushing feverishly into a consuming flame. It is not that you are becoming weaker, less potent, less ambitious, more lonely as the years affirm their grip and one by one those closest to you vanish, leaving scars upon your soul. I think it is simply that death has a gravitational pull. It habitually demonstrates its power against yet another inevitable victim. And when the victim has chosen the time and means for his departure, the power of that gravitational pull is hastened as the known climactic moment nears.

Many things are known about suicide. More suicides occur in daytime than at night and their number grows as the seasonal solstice lengthens the duration of light. Also, oddly enough, the first four days of a week are more tempting for self-immolation than the last three; no one knows why. The effect of wind has been remarked upon. In the Mediterranean the south wind is the most suicidal. In whatever land, moreover, the hottest season of the year is generally the one which makes for murder of one's own person.

The more cultivated a person is intellectually, the more likely he is to kill himself, according to mathematical analysis. Authors have an abnormally high inclination: among many, Gérard de Nerval, Heinrich von Kleist, Vladimir Mayakovsky, Hart Crane, Virginia Woolf, and Ernest Hemingway.

Long-enduring customs and traditions play a frequent role in suicide. Romanticists during various phases of literature have chosen this method of terminating the lives of their heroes and heroines. Madame de Staël said of Goethe's *Werther* that it had caused more suicides than the most beautiful woman in the world. The Japanese, since time immemorial, have considered this an honorable, ritualistic end, cutting their own throats until the eighth century and subsequently moving down the body to *seppuku* — disembowelment with a ceremonial short saber.

Seneca, to whom I so often refer as having extolled a man's

control over his own death, ended his days by slicing his veins while seated in a warm bath that made his blood flow more strongly, saying that to die was a means of escaping a bad life. Zenon the Stoic justified suicide in Athens during the fourth century B.C. and Epicurus of Samos, who founded a rival philosophical school, likewise approved the act.

Gods of Scandinavian and German mythology, Odin, Frigga, and Helgo, slew themselves as did many subsequent kings who practiced their pagan faith. Both the Hindus and the Eskimos, who believe in reincarnation as metempsychosis, consequently have no strong prejudice against suicide and it is prevalent among them.

Montaigne recommended "voluntary death" as the most beautiful; Nietzsche extolled it because it was his "wish"; Voltaire said only people with souls employed this "refinement"; Balzac called it a "sublime poem"; Homer considered it a "natural act"; Kant called it the "supreme revolt"; and Dostoyevsky argued that once one had lost the "idea of immortality" the thought of suicide became "a necessity, inevitable and absolute."

I have a special respect for and interest in Karl Marx's daughter, Laura, and her Communist husband, Paul Lafargue. They swore not to live beyond the biblical age of three score years and ten. When they passed that barrier, Lafargue wrote a note saying he was of sound mind and body but was killing himself because "pitiless age" was depriving him, one by one, of the joys of existence and paralyzing his energy, his physical and intellectual force. He and his wife injected cyanide into their veins but he thoughtfully wrote a postscript to his death note requesting that the person who took over their dog should love him and not beat him. For me and Christopher, who are a team, that would be insufficient reassurance.

It is strange that when one contemplates an act which has total significance, one's memory automatically recollects associated bits and pieces of information related to such action. I have no gift for quick remembrance. It takes my slow mind time to reassort its complex filing cabinet. Yet when it has finally arranged the intellectual input of a lifetime, and is powerfully concentrated by the imminence of an awful deed, much filters through the sclerotic mechanism of the brain.

Over and over I find myself harking back to the classics when I think of suicide, its morality and consequences; not its method, which is easy. I believe it was again Seneca who pointed out that, as one takes care to select a good boat on which to embark for a voyage and a good house in which to dwell, it is likewise just that one should have the right to choose the means of ending one's life. In death even more than in other things, the wise Roman reasoned, we should follow our own individual taste.

Centuries before Seneca, Timon of Athens hanged himself on his fig tree, which was so large and strong that many other Athenians had already used it for the same purpose, a fact that did not greatly disturb the philosopher, who tended to misanthropy. There are many, many fig trees on Spetsais.

Do all these recollections of the thoughts of famous people seem to you doleful and melancholic? Is it death itself, or the manner of achieving it, that brings such sadness to so many? And what can be less sad than an aesthetically "well-crafted" termination of the experience of life, an end accompanied by the companion who knows and loves me best, just as the splendor of dawn bursts over the ageless Aegean grandeur?

Now as I row, as the oarlocks squeal and the clumsy old boat heads ever southward, there are no more lights ashore save two occasionally revolving distant pharoses. But overhead, while the moon slips speedily onward, the stars assume a special and burning bright benevolence. They reflect down upon us so we can see quite clearly.

Christopher has ceased looking with puzzlement at the phosphorescent ripples of the oar blades and the gurgling wake. He stares into my eyes and I see the twinkling of the stars in his.

And he regards the strange assortment of tools and artifacts I have assembled to accomplish our joint purpose: the rusted old anchors, the chains coiled before my feet, the thick cork floating plank, and the gun behind me in the bow; above all the gun. Christopher has never gone shooting; he hates the noise. But he knows there is something unholy about a gun. Two days ago, he watched me oiling it and cleaning it. He did not like what he saw.

I have a weird suspicion that his special intuitive apparatus sometimes tells him things that are at least equivalent in import to what mankind's pretensions to intellect advise. On the one hand his heart is so pure (if mischief be excepted), so loyal, and so fragile that he could not conceivably question my decision to take him with me on the longest journey, the instant trip across eternity's threshold. Yet, is he not also aware in a mysterious way of what Robert Burton, citing Ovid, wrote in his great book:

> Our life is short and tedious, and in the death of a man there is no recovery, neither was any man known that hath returned from the grave: for we are born at all adventure, and we shall be hereafter as though we had never been; for the breath is as smoke in our nostrils and the spirit vanisheth as the soft Air.

Paw in hand, we prepare to face this nothingness together.

XVIII Shortly before the eastern sky turned gray and the soughing early morning breeze began to murmur upward from the south, I reached our approximate destination. It had been a long row over the increasingly rippled waves that caressed the eight-centuries-old wrecks of *Sette Pozzi*, resting on the sand so many fathoms below. I reckoned a south wind was favorable to our enterprise, for any remaining flotsam that escaped its final act would drift far away, past the rock-spit called Widow of Sharks, and probably disappear without a trace off the cliff-walled Peloponnesian shore.

As I looked northward and westward at the bare outline of retreating Spetsais in the distance I thought of the whitewashed courtyards of its little houses; the fig, pomegranate, orange, lemon, pine, and cypress trees; the pastel-colored flowers of spring; the birds rippling in the branches of mountain copses; the clicking of cicadas; and the slight surf-borne fleece blowing across the rocky coasts. Above all I thought of that poem written so many years ago by Odysseus Elytis and called "Marina of the Rocks":

> Deep in the gold of summer
> And the perfume of hyacinths
> But where did you wander
> Descending toward the shores
> The pebbled bays . . .

These words are graven on my heart and, in both Greek and English, on each side of the portal of our house.

"One must weep for men at their birth and at their death," wrote Montesquiou, a sentiment with which I do not agree in either sense. At their birth only the newly-born weep, and it is in truth a paean of joy which also has the benevolent effect of filling their lungs with the goodness of air. Those present smile with pleasure. And at death, it is not for the dead that one must weep but for their survivors. The dead have nothing to mourn; they are incapable of any memory. Yet, if they have lived good or sweet or generous lives, those they leave behind indeed have reason to weep, pining for what is irreparably gone and also, as is alas the frequent case, for the fear of what awaits their own selves.

Greece, which gave so much of life to this world, is a peculiar place to die; far less suitable, for example than Egypt. The ancient Greeks were not in the least obsessed with death as were the even more ancient Egyptians. From Proto-Helladic times right on to Aristotle, the Greeks weren't even of the same opinion as to what death was. They located the souls of its victims in Hades across the River Styx in a Peloponnesian cave.

The Greeks love life; but on their own terms. I believe virtually all of them would die within a week if they had no one to talk to, argue with, or share their vague appreciation for the very sound of another Greek voice. But the Egyptians, although a highly pragmatic people, have always venerated death with their own special brand of mysticism and a kind of eager appreciation. The Theban *Book of the Dead*, more than thirty centuries ago, was reminding priest and layman alike:

> Millions of years have gone over the world; I cannot tell the number of those through which thou hast passed. . . . May I come unto the land of eternity, may I come even unto the everlasting land, for behold, O my lord, this thou hast ordained for me. . . .
>
> My soul shall not be fettered to my body at the gates of the underworld; but I shall enter in peace and I shall come forth in peace. . . . I am he who cometh forth, advancing, whose name is unknown. . . . I am he who is never overwhelmed in the waters. Happy, yea happy, is the funeral couch of the Still-Heart. . . .
>
> Hail, I have become helpless: Hail, I have become helpless: but I go forward. . . . At night taketh place the festival of him that is dead, the Aged One, who is in ward (in) the earth. . . . I am the lord of light and that which is an abomination to me is death. . . . I have overthrown mine enemies upon earth, and yet my perishable body is in the grave. . . . The duration of thy life shall be for ever, and thy sovereignty shall be everlasting, and thy periods of one hundred and twenty years shall be endless.

Christopher, whose eyes are clearly visible, mirroring the approach of dawn, regards me with bewilderment as he sniffs the morning with its scudding droplets of salt. He has some appreciation of the gravity of our terminal moments and a certain air of apprehension, as if he were inquiring: "Do you think we will see God?"

I tell him in all earnestness: "I won't. I don't believe in Him. I don't think He ever did exist. But maybe you will. You think all nice humans are gods. Like Marina. And the children. And even me.

"I won't see God but I imagine what God looks like. She is dark grey with many rubbery arms like an enormous octopus. But if there are angels with God they have long brown ears, glowing black eyes, wet palpitating noses, skin like the softest velvet, and white curling tails. They will be your friends and playmates forever. Of course, you think forever means just today. And maybe you are right."

Now behind us in the distance the olive trees are emerging with a particular silvery color as greyness lightens over Hydra far away, pointing to the sun's expected diurnal course. Everywhere there is a stirring and even out at sea, laboring with awkward oars, one can feel the bursting, turbulent, terrific Greek spring.

Christopher sits there patiently on the tossing board-seat in the stern: a timid little dog with a mighty bark that strikes fear among Greeks. Poor fellow: he loved my wife quite as much as I — and she him. After her death I simply had to double the intensity of my love for him in order to make his life bearable. Never for an instant could I have contemplated forcing him to endure once again the terrible and traumatic shock of losing everything.

When I gazed with overwhelming sorrow at my small friend I reflected on how we both lived with and among increasingly incomprehensible forces created by ourselves: mindless computer memories; death-dealing, life-preserving laser beams; the knowledge that an atom is to its contained if undiscoverable components as large as the universe compared to any one of us.

Not even our most secret dreams are proof against pseudoscientific inquiry; far better to forget them. I doubt if Christopher is in any tangible way aware of these complex factors, despite his extraordinary perceptive talents; but he is caught up in them just as inextricably as I and perhaps only because of and through me.

I reflected furthermore — and this most assuredly could in no way have been shared by Christopher — that the amount of space we traverse is ultimately limited, no matter how endless it may seem. Only time is limitless. Christopher has never even conceived of time as an abstract entity. If I go away for a week, a day, or an hour he is mournful and I receive from him the same ecstatic homecoming welcome whether my absence has been relatively long or short. The only time of which he has an approximate idea is lunchtime, the one meal a day he is allowed.

Time, I pondered, is impassive and without measure and in the latter sense the little beagle is shrewder and wiser than I give him credit for. Only as a human becomes old does time seem to accelerate its speed. Yet in fact there is no change; nor has there ever been. It is merely that time may seem to be penetrated at different rates. The supersonic plane or intercontinental missile are speedier than the tortoise — unless he is riding in one or the other himself. But they are incredibly slower than a ray of light.

Alexander Woollcott, a brilliant talker, used to speculate that men who loved dogs were perhaps atoning for some consciously forgotten cruelty toward fellow humans. He spoke of a once-fashionable theory of psychiatrists that such an affection for four-footed friends is a telltale token of an old brutality undergoing compensation; or at least might be an outward scar of an ancient impulse of cruelty toward mankind, "never satisfied, perhaps, and long since suppressed." But Woollcott was more of a talker than a thinker or writer, and great talkers almost invariably do not know their own thoughts until they hear them issuing from their mouths.

I at least know whereof I speak with respect to myself. I know I am curmudgeonly, but I do not remember having committed major acts of which I needed greatly to be ashamed. Yet by the time I was an old man, I found my circle of genuine friends had been squeezed down to one small beagle whom I adored. He depended on me and I on him; thus we were true equals. Under any but the most exiguous occasions I refused to leave him and I never permitted him to remain alone except when he chose to run away in carefree happiness or to explore the mysteries he was forever discovering in life.

Nor would I even accept the tendency of most airlines to consign him to a baggage hold when carrying us from one point to another. Always he sat beside me or at my feet and on occasion, because of his bedroom eyes, some kindly stewardess would serve him — alone among the passengers in economy class — a portion of caviar, which he adores. This unusual occurrence invariably provoked howls of protest from the two-legged beasts accompanying us.

It is entirely fitting that our last journey should be peaceful, intimate, and solitary — a suitable conclusion to our last years of intimate and solitary life. Once I was with an uncle of whom I was extremely fond when he suffered a stroke in Burma — at an age younger than mine is at this journey's end. He was kept alive, paralyzed and disconsolate for a full decade, the wreckage of a man of vigor and intelligence who retained his probing brain but no other vestige of his real self for ten unhappy years before merciful death arrived.

None of that for Christopher or myself. We prefer to depart existence as integral, active creatures. Today, thanks to the obscene discoveries of warped medical science, it is possible to preserve what is called life in bodies that are in all but the legal sense already dead. By mechanical devices and artificial or grafted organs, humans have been pickled for long periods after they were no longer conscious or, if they were, no longer wished to be. They assumed a vegetable existence, wired to tubes and batteries and tended by nurses and physicians imagining this was a kindly and benevolent deed.

For us there will be no risk of such embarrassment. My children are well, happy, and occupied: a daughter busy with her excellent husband and a pair of extraordinary children; my son passionately taken up with his highly specialized business that fascinates him and keeps him endlessly traveling, which he adores. Despite their love, both Christopher and I feel increasingly alone. This is the commonplace melancholia of age and I have decided for the sake of both of us to indulge such final weakness.

After all, to be afraid of death is insanity. It is the logical equivalent of being afraid of never having been born. To be afraid of dying is different; too many of my friends have suffered the protracted and desperate agonies of cancer, the bewilderment of paralysis or the helplessness of senility for all too long a time before expiring. Decrepitude, at all costs, should be avoided for both man and man's best friends.

As I sway backward and forward clasping the thick-handled, stubby oars, Christopher's face emerges more and more accurately as the full light preliminary to the sun itself sweeps over us on the sighing offshore wind. His eyes are shining and, as always, rendered still more beautiful by seeming to be rimmed with black kohl, like those of the lovely central Asian houris whose religious creed insists their faces and figures be shrouded save for the eyes.

Knowing that he does not really understand the meaning of the word but nevertheless wishes to be advised and consulted on any important event concerning us, I explain to Christopher that suicide is precisely the same kind of act and for precisely the same purpose as putting down a favorite dog to avoid its further suffering, an act with which he fortunately is not familiar. But I was the favorite dog to be put down and he was my chosen companion to step across the threshold of eternity.

After all, I recall that three of my friends, all fine, intelligent and active men, chose to end their own lives with shotguns when they found their talents vanishing and their senses failing: Frank Wisner, who would have been head of the CIA; Phil Graham, brilliant publisher of the *Washington Post* and *Newsweek;* and Ernest Hemingway, who discovered to his horror that it had become impossible for him to write any longer. The shotgun is an efficient and instantaneous tool for self-immolation, if intolerably messy for survivors forced to clean up the remains. With us there will be no such grimy task. Death in the Aegean Sea has a lovely, clean anonymity. I had always preferred for myself the idea of a watery end, long before I first contemplated suicide some time after Marina's untimely end brought sad reality into our lives.

There are still a vast number of people who would escape lifelessness by weirdly preserving themselves, either mummified or else ultimately as skeletons, in the hope that these grisly relics might at least be used as the basis for a form of physical resurrection. How peculiar that mankind at some early date conceived the idea of saving shriveled bodies or bleached bones. Why on earth should such remnants be consigned to cathedrals, ossuaries, vaults, or catacombs simply because the bone is a portion of the body which outlasts the rest by containing a larger proportion of lime? Would it not be equally sensible to immortalize memories in piles of human ordure, marinated brains, hair, or fingernails?

I intend to leave nothing; nothing but recollections of two meager creatures, one of whom, Christopher, was loved wholeheartedly by almost everyone he ever knew. There will be no note, no explanation. There will be no religious or other memorial for, over three decades, I have left formal instructions with members of my family, friends, secretaries, lawyers that I wish no tombstone or other totem when I die.

The only problem is to insure that our two bodies vanish utterly and forever below the waves. When the little skiff that bears us across our own River Styx eventually winds up empty on some Peloponnesian shore, days later, it will bear no trace of what has happened to us, no speck of blood, no memory leading to unhappy but not miserable speculation by those familiar with my passion for very long swims and Christopher's eagerness, somehow or other, to follow where I go.

Only one grim detail is essential. Our corpses, either whole or piecemeal, must never, never again be washed to the surface. I learned in my first year of newspaper work, forty-six years ago in Pittsburgh, when covering the county morgue as a reporter, that aqueous corpses are unpleasant. We kept them in what was called the Floaters' Tank when they were hauled out of the city's three splendidly named rivers: Monongahela, Alleghany, and Ohio. And there I — aged barely twenty-two — was instructed by coroners that it is difficult to gauge how long a body has been under water but the longer, the less pleasant, on the whole. Contributory factors include physical condition, temperature of the water, and its organic content. Generally speaking, the fingers acquire what was called a "washday" appearance after about three hours. After two days pronounced swelling of the palms develops; five days of immersion turns them chalky white. It is difficult at first to tell whether what was always called the "deceased" was dead or alive when immersed. However, an autopsy showed whether lungs contained water, sand, or particles of vegetable matter; no one can inhale when dead.

But this is no problem facing Christopher and me. At the very moment the sun's fierce orange rim slips above the island of Hydra and a tender rosy path extends ever further over the lapping waves, caressing us as it passes, I cease straining at the oars and prepare for our quick chaotic bundling into eternity.

"Have no fear, Christopher," I murmur, reaching down for the plank of cork. "The sea is a gentle and impassive resting place: clean, secret, cool, and with its own arcane rhythm. You have always liked the sea."

The cork has a heavy string attached to it, drawn through a

tiny hole, so that the string may be removed by a single yank. It floats well even on water that is not entirely smooth as it is almost five inches thick and can bear a considerable burden buoyantly.

I reach forward for Christopher, having first shipped the oars, and talking softly and endearingly to him all the time cover the little body with his favorite, ragged blue towel in which so many hundreds of times I have dried him off and rubbed him down following one of his joyful swims. It is an object of great sentimental meaning to him. He regards it as a toy, often dragging it from his chair in the house and rushing around waving it frantically, furious mock growls emerging from his wagging head. He accepts the towel with gratitude and reassurance as I draw him to me.

Then, most gently in order not to frighten him, enclosed in his towel, I wrap around him a long, moderately heavy steel chain with strong snap-hooks at each end. I tie it quite firmly but not so tight that he cannot move with ease, crossing it twice along the length of his small, sturdy shape and three times around his girth. Then I attach a pair of iron anchors with pointed tips at each fluke. He looks bewildered and a bit afraid, more I suspect because of the sadness and gravity of my expression and my touch than because of the curious things I am doing.

When all this has been accomplished, I place the cork plank in the water, tying the attaching cord around the port oarlock. It bobs well above the lapping ripples as I lift Christopher, suddenly struggling with an abrupt surge of fear, and place him on the raft, last resting place of his life, the two anchors near one edge so they will help tip the apparatus when necessary.

I shove it two feet away from the drifting boat, open my gun case rapidly, fit the stock to the twin over-and-under barrel, and suddenly lean over the side with it so that I can aim parallel and even slightly upward at the despairing target. Thus I shall avoid piercing the cork with even a single telltale shot that might lend a hint of suspicion to its condition when and if it ever floats ashore, all bloodstains long ago washed off by the briny waves.

Since childhood, I have not once cried except when I laid my head beside the agonized features of Marina after she died six years ago. However, now great tears roll down my cheeks as, looking into his suddenly bewildered eyes I point the muzzle at his darling head from only twelve inches distance. Just far enough away to insure immediate result and avoid a splattering on the rowboat, I blow off the head of my beloved Christopher. Blinded by my tears I help the anchors overturn the raft and the little beagle disappears forever. I jerk the string and the cork slides over him into the endless flow of jetsam the sea has always borne.

I then cast overboard my own swimming towel and moccasins, bush shirt and blue jeans. I am confident that whatever eventually becomes of them they will add no understanding to those few who survive me and are interested, who assuredly will assume we drowned together by tragic accident. Only partially wrong: it was in a worldly sense tragic but in no sense an accident.

I take the heavier, longer chain and bring it up between my legs and over my shoulders, wrap it twice about my neck and then bring it downward, twice girdling my waist and tying it tightly at the ends with two thick but astoundingly pliable strands of wire, one of copper, one of steel, wound round and round like hangman's knots, which indeed they truly are. Then to the huge snaphook by my feet I attach a large, fifty-pound anchor. To the snaphook at my waist I attach another of half that size. Together with the weight of the iron chain links and my gun, which I now tie to the chain by a lengthy double strand of copper wire run through its trigger guard so it will remain attached to me forever, I reckon that almost my poundage in long-enduring metal will bear me to the sandy bottom I know lies along the galleon battlefield below and will hold me there ever more tightly as my flesh disintegrates and dwindles.

Then I hang the two anchors over the port side of the boat, the side where Christopher has just died. I clamber into the soft water, hanging onto the thwart with one hand and directing the gun muzzle toward me with the other, holding it in my open mouth. Once it is firmly there I can clasp it tightly and clamp my teeth over the terminal sight while my hand, now freed from the barrel, gropes upward to the trigger.

It is entirely wrong to believe as many people do that in the last instant before eternity one reviews one's entire life at blazing speed. I do not see the dearest, compassionate face of Marina. I think of no gaiety nor any tragedy during my seven decades of existence. I do not even see the adoring, trustful eyes of Christopher, my closest companion whom I murdered. As my finger crooks itself around the catch, I see only the blazing heliotropic sun, now sliding silently overhead; a sun that was here for eons before I noticed it and will remain for eons afterward, never having noticed me. Quite rightly.

And I pull the trigger.